ANXIETY AND STRESS MANAGEMENT

Most stress is a normal part of daily life, and can be coped with adequately by the individual. Prolonged or more serious stress however may require professional help. A local GP can often provide this but in many cases will refer the client to a mental health worker or other health professional. *Anxiety and Stress Management* is written for each of these groups: as a practical handbook and guide for those professionals working in the field of mental health, but also written for the referring GP and those seeking help themselves.

The authors integrate theoretical and academic material relating to anxiety and stress research with clinical experience. The book begins with a theoretical section offering a working model of stress, a guide to diagnostic classification, and alternative models of anxiety. This is followed by chapters on assessment, explaining the problem and treatment procedures to the client, teaching specific self-help skills, and changing stressful lifestyles. Advice is also given on running anxiety and stress management groups, and individual case studies are examined. The authors make extensive use of analogy and metaphor to ensure ready understanding and recall. They also include many useful inventories, questionnaires, charts, and client handouts.

Anxiety and Stress Management will be of use to all health professionals working with people who have anxiety and stress related problems, but will prove equally valuable for the clients themselves as a reference book and as a means of self-education and self-help.

STRATEGIES FOR MENTAL HEALTH

Series editor

Reinhard Kowalski

Principal Clinical Psychologist and Psychotherapist,
East Berkshire Health Authority
and
The Cardinal Clinic, Windsor, Berkshire

STRATEGIES FOR MENTAL HEALTH is a series of guide books for the mental health practitioner. It will introduce practitioners to relevant therapeutic approaches in a practical 'hands on' way. Over recent years numerous psychological therapy approaches to mental health have been developed and many of them have become well-established methods in the field. The dilemma that practitioners and students face is how to obtain an up-to-date practice-orientated introduction to a particular method without having to work their way through a mass of research literature.

The books in this series are written by experienced practitioners and trainers. Style and content are practice-orientated, giving readers the knowledge, skills, and materials needed to plan, set up, and run projects in their particular area of mental health work. Those who want to acquire a deeper knowledge of the theoretical foundations will find up-to-date references with each one of the titles.

Already published

REHABILITATION AND COMMUNITY CARE
Stephen Pilling

Forthcoming titles

ASSERTIVENESS TRAINING
Shân Rees and Roderick S. Graham

BEREAVEMENT AND LOSS
David Jeffrey

ANXIETY AND STRESS MANAGEMENT

TREVOR J. POWELL

and

SIMON J. ENRIGHT

LONDON AND NEW YORK

First published in 1990
Reprinted in paperback in 1991 and 1993
by Routledge
11 New Fetter Lane, London EC4P 4EE

Simultaneously published in the USA and Canada
by Routledge
29 West 35th Street, New York, NY 10001

Typeset by J&L Composition Ltd, Filey, North Yorkshire
Printed and bound in Great Britain by
Biddles Ltd, Guildford and King's Lynn

British Library Cataloguing in Publication Data

Powell, Trevor J., 1955–
Anxiety and stress management.
1. Man. Stress
I. Title   II. Enright, Simon J., 1960–
155.9

Library of Congress Cataloging in Publication Data
Also available

ISBN 0–415–04457–X
0–415–01069–1 (pbk)

CONTENTS

ILLUSTRATIONS

ACKNOWLEDGEMENTS

We would like to express our sincere thanks to Mrs Sheila Watkinson and Mrs Ann Dellis for their patience and skill in typing the early drafts and completed manuscript.

Trevor Powell
Simon Enright

PREFACE

This book has been written primarily as a practical guide for health professionals working with clients experiencing anxiety and stress-related problems. We have attempted to explain theoretical ideas in everyday language, avoiding the use of jargon and relying on metaphor and analogy to assist understanding and recall. The authors hope that health workers may wish to use the explanations and techniques presented to supplement their own clinical practice and to help clarify their own ideas on anxiety and stress.

Our clinical approach is largely a cognitive–behavioural one; the aim of our therapeutic interventions being to help the client to understand and demystify symptoms, to teach new coping skills and to encourage lifestyle changes where necessary. The book also includes a number of client handouts, record forms, diary sheets, and assessment procedures which we have found useful in our own clinical practice. We would like to acknowledge that many of these therapeutic aids have been acquired from others throughout the course of our clinical experience. As such, we would like to state our appreciation to those numerous clinicians, and invite readers to adopt and use these aids as they wish.

Though the book has been written principally with health professionals in mind, we hope that the style and contents of the book will prove equally readable and useful for the clients themselves to use as a reference book and a means of self-education and self-help. Although this book has been a collaboration, Trevor Powell has been the main contributor to chapters 1, 3, 6, 7 and Simon Enright to chapters 2, 4, 5, 8.

EDITOR'S INTRODUCTION

The field of ANXIETY AND STRESS MANAGEMENT has grown in recent years. While the problem of stress has become more widely recognized in our society, clinical psychologists and others have set out to investigate the relationship between stress and mental health more closely. As a result a wide range of treatment methods has developed, and anxiety and stress management is now practised throughout the health service and beyond. This guidebook is written by two clinical psychologists, and it aims in a particularly comprehensive way at providing readers with the tools to set up their own anxiety and stress management projects. Hence it serves as a practice-orientated introduction for the learner, and a source of skills and materials for the more experienced practitioner.

In chapter one Powell and Enright summarize theories of stress and provide the reader with some useful questionnaires to assess life events, job stress, and Type-A behaviour. Chapter two tries to bring some order into the different classification systems and theories of anxiety in a user-friendly way. Chapter three describes the cognitive-behavioural assessment procedure for stress and anxiety management. A special feature is the practical examples and the assessment sheets and questionnaires which the authors use in their own clinical work. Chapter four looks at the process of education in anxiety and stress management. Readers can easily adapt the explanations of stress, anxiety, panic attacks, and the rationale for a cognitive-behavioural treatment approach which are found in this chapter for their own therapy practice. Chapter five deals with techniques like relaxation, controlling hyperventilation, distraction, etc. All the techniques are presented 'ready for use'. Chapter six deals with helping clients to change their lifestyles and covers important areas like goal planning, assertiveness, and social support. Chapter seven gives the format for running an anxiety management group. It contains a wealth of sound clinical advice and it summarizes recent research findings. In chapter eight Powell and Enright present comprehensive case examples from their clinical practice, covering stress, agoraphobia, post traumatic stress disorder, panic attacks, and phobias. Each case example is highly structured and includes a description of the assessment procedure, the problem formulation, and the treatment process and outcome.

This guidebook on anxiety and stress management is relevant for those whose orientation is cognitive-behavioural as well as for practitioners who adhere to different models. Cognitive and behavioural therapies have become sophisticated enough to claim the 'psychotherapy' label, while many other therapy approaches are searching for a more practical and reality-orientated context. The practical orientation of this guidebook can form the bridge for practitioners of different schools of thought who are interested in anxiety and stress management.

Reinhard Kowalski

Chapter One

WHAT WE KNOW ABOUT STRESS – A MODEL BASED ON RESEARCH

INTRODUCTION

Everybody experiences stress in their lives, from the rural Scottish crofter, to the suburban mother, to the high-flyer business executive. Throughout history people have experienced stress – it is part and parcel of the human condition as chronicled in art and literature throughout the ages.

The pervasiveness of stress in our society is evident in the variety of ways our language is able to express it; you might say, 'I feel wound up/under strain/under pressure/tense/panicky/ uptight/agitated'. Whatever phrase we may use, stress happens to us all.

The stress of everyday life shows itself in lots of ways: an angry snapped reply to an innocent question, a pounding headache at the end of a hard day at work, the driver drumming their fingers on the steering wheel in a traffic jam. These daily stresses are normal. However, with prolonged and more serious stress people often begin to develop troublesome symptoms which they worry about. It is at this point that they might look for outside help, and often the first port of call is the local general practitioner. In most cases the doctor will offer help, reassurance, and possibly even medication. In some cases where the individual is coping inadequately, they will be referred on to a mental health worker or a community mental health team – usually consisting of such professionals as clinical psychologists, psychiatrists, social workers, occupational therapists, counsellors, and community psychiatric nurses. This book is written as a clinical resource and practical guide for those professionals, but will also be useful as a handbook for the clients themselves and any member of the public with an interest in self-help methods of managing stress.

THE SIZE OF THE PROBLEM

Although people have experienced stress throughout history, there is evidence to suggest that the problems associated with stress have escalated during the twentieth century, particularly in highly developed westernized countries. Let us pause to consider a few statistics which will put the problem of stress in context (see Figure 1.1).

Figure 1.1   The size of the problem: a few statistics

1 An estimated 80 per cent of all modern diseases have their beginnings in stress.
2 In the early 1980s 1 in 10 adult British males and 1 in 5 adult British females received prescriptions for the benzodiazepine class of tranquillizer.
3 4–5 per cent of the population are treated for diagnosed anxiety complaints each year.
4 In Britain 250,000 people die annually due to coronary heart disease (the most common cause of death) – the death rate doubled for men aged 34–44 between 1953 and 1973.
5 40 million days are lost to British industry every year due to direct stress related conditions (as accounted for by NHS certificates).
6 A conservative estimate of the cost of stress to British industry would be £1.3 billion a year. Typical symptoms would include alcoholism, absenteeism, premature death, and retirement.
7 In the USA there has been a 500 per cent increase in coronary heart disease over the last fifty years.
8 In the USA 8 million people have stomach ulcers. 12 million people are estimated to have alcohol problems.
9 Americans take 5 billion doses of tranquillizers and 16,000 tons of aspirin each year.

What is the explanation for the increase in these stress related conditions? A commonly held view is that the 'pace of life' has increased. Sociologists might identify factors such as the decline of traditional structures such as community networks and extended families, the decline of commonly held values, beliefs, and rituals incorporated in traditional religions, changing working practices, greater social and geographical mobility, poor diet, lack of exercise, the restrictive medicalization of symptoms, or even the fact that we are now more vigilant record keepers. All these factors have been linked with trying to explain the increase in reported stress related problems. It seems likely that there is some truth in all these arguments. However, although it is important to be aware of these issues, sociological discussion about the causes of stress are beyond the scope of the book.

A WORKING MODEL OF STRESS

Before contemplating any form of therapeutic intervention it is important to have an understanding or a model of stress. This model is very much like a map of the general landscape giving us direction and helping us to see our way forward. All of us carry around in our heads some form of idiosyncratic model of stress; some people's models or ideas may be more sophisticated, complex, or explicit than others. For the purpose of this book it is important to articulate that model at an early stage as it is the basis for understanding all that follows.

Before examining our model let us first attempt to define the subject of that model, namely the term stress. Lazarus gives us the following formal definition of stress: 'stress refers to a broad class of problems differentiated from other problem areas because it deals with any demands which tax the system, whatever it is, a physiological system, a social system or a psychological system and the response of that system' (Lazarus 1971: 53–60). He goes on to say that the 'reaction depends on how the person interprets or appraises (consciously or unconsciously) the significance of a harmful, threatening or challenging event' (ibid.).

This definition contains three important components for a model of stress:

1 The idea of demands taxing a system.
2 The idea that there is some form of appraisal or perception of threat.
3 The importance of the response of that system.

The notion of demands taxing an individual or a system implies a temporary state of unbalance or disequilibrium. These demands are not just a result of external forces acting on a point, as in the case in the engineering definition of stress,

3

rather they are the result of the interaction between external forces and the internal factors which make up an individual or system. Both these external environmental factors and internal individual factors can be further broken down into a number of separate categories. Empirical research has demonstrated that each of these categories have a significant part to play in the process of stress (see Figure 1.2). A circular or trans-actional relationship exists between the individual and their environment – both influence and effect each other. Out of this transactional relationship develop different states of equilibrium and disequilibrium or imbalance. This process does not go on unnoticed as some form of conscious, or unconscious, judge-ment is being made continuously. This judgement or perception of threat is largely determined by factors which make up an individual, such as one's thoughts, attitudes, past experiences, temperament, physical make-up, and factors in the environ-ment. This perception of threat will influence the resultant state of stress, which will manifest itself in different areas of physical, cognitive, and behavioural symptoms. The individual or system will react to this state of stress in an attempt to restore equili-brium. This reaction is important as it directly affects the future abilities and character of the individual. Some reactions can be viewed as adaptive as they move the system on to a further state of equilibrium, reducing overall demands. Other reactions could be viewed as maladaptive as they create further secondary problems which adversely affect the future of the individual.

The model of stress is very similar to the notion of homeo-stasis in the natural world as elaborated by Cannon (1929). Stated simply: a system or individual when unbalanced will strive to re-establish equilibrium. Sometimes that system or in-dividual may need help and this is the underlying basis of anxiety and stress management counselling. The model offers a compre-hensive framework for incorporating and understanding all stress related problems. The rest of this chapter will examine and explain further the different individual components of the model.

THE ENVIRONMENT

Life Events

A considerable body of work, originating from the research of Holmes and Rahe (1967), suggests that certain life events that

Figure 1.2 A working model of stress

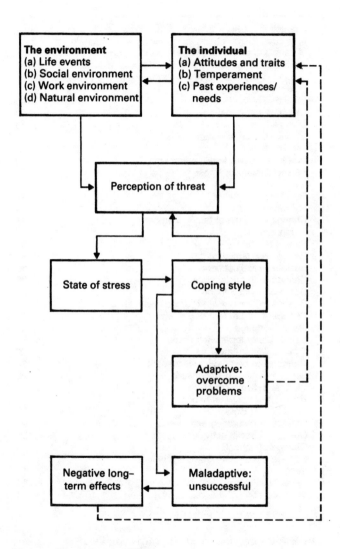

Source: Adapted from Cooper (1981)

Figure 1.3   The Holmes–Rahe Life Stress Inventory

Instructions: Check off each of the following life events that has happened to you during the previous year. Total up your score. A score of over 300 points in one year greatly increases your risk of a stress-related health problem. A score of below 150 means a relatively low amount of life change and a low susceptibility to stress induced breakdown.

LIFE EVENT	LIFE CHANGE UNITS
Death of a spouse	100
Divorce	73
Marital-relationship separation	65
Imprisonment	63
Death of a close family member	63
Personal injury or illness	53
Marriage	50
Dismissal from work	47
Retirement	45
Change in health of family member	44
Pregnancy	40
Sexual difficulties	39
Gain a new family member	39
Business readjustment	39
Change in financial state	38
Death of a close friend	37
Change in number of arguments with spouse	35
Change to a different line of work	34
Major mortgage	32
Son or daughter leaving home	29
Trouble with in-laws	29
Outstanding personal achievement	28
Spouse begins or stops work	26
Change in living conditions	25
Revision of personal habits	23
Trouble with Boss	22
Change in recreation activities	21
Change in social activities	20
Change of schools	20
Change in number of family reunions	15
Vacation	13
Christmas	12
Minor violation of the law	11

cause change, increase an individual's susceptibility to stress-related illness. In a number of studies, they weighted particular life events on a scale from 0 to 100 and looked at a selected heterogeneous population sample, both prospectively and retro-spectively (see Figure 1.3). These life events involved change of some kind, including changes in health, family relationships, economic and living conditions, education, religion, and social affairs. They ranged in severity from major life crises, such as death of a spouse, to relatively minor events, like going on holiday or receiving a parking ticket. Each individual was given a total life change score for a given period of time. They found that individuals with high life change scores were more likely to have a stress related illness during the following two year period.

Correlational studies suggest a relationship between life change scores and the onset of tuberculosis, heart disease, skin diseases, a general deterioration in health, and poorer academic performance. Further studies found a relationship with psychiatric symptomatology; a net increase in life events was associated with worsening of symptoms and a net decrease with improvement. These researchers contend that it is the nature of change itself which is stressful, regardless of whether it is perceived as favourable or unfavourable.

In another study looking at changing lifestyle Syme (1966) concluded that men and women whose life situation is significantly different from that in which they grew up have an increased risk of heart attacks. For a farm boy who moves to a large city and takes a 'white collar' job there is an increased risk of 300 per cent. If he takes a 'blue collar' job the risk is considerably less.

Social Environment

Many researchers (Cassel 1976, Ganster and Victor 1988) have argued that people who are part of an extensive social network are less negatively affected by stressful life events and are less likely to experience stress related health problems. It is also widely maintained that naturally existing support systems, such as extended families, work groups, and communities, facilitate better coping, rehabilitation, and recovery. It has been hypothesized that social support serves as a buffer or mediator between life stresses and poor health.

The term social support refers to personal contact available to an individual from other individuals or groups. This contact produces a number of obvious benefits:

1 The individual is provided with a means of expressing his or her feelings.
2 Feedback from others is important in helping to develop an appropriate appraisal of a situation and realistic goals, also helping the person establish a sense of meaning.
3 Social contacts can also provide useful information and practical help.

A number of studies have suggested that people who live alone and who are not involved with other people or organizations are more vulnerable to a variety of stress related chronic illnesses. Lynch (1977) argued that the socially isolated die prematurely. He compared mortality figures indicating that married people experience a lower mortality rate (from all diseases) than unmarried people. Research studies have shown that members of certain religious groups have lower incidence of stress-related health problems, attributed to their tightly knit and cohesive communities. In many cases it is not the quantity of contacts but the quality or relationship. One study, Brown and Harris (1978), showed that women who had one important confiding relationship with a husband, lover, or friend, were 90 per cent less likely to become depressed than women who had no such relationship to rely on.

Work Environment

An aspect of life that has received much attention from researchers is work. Apart from providing financial income, work can satisfy a number of basic human needs – mental and physical exercise, social contact, feelings of self worth, confidence, and competence. However, work can also be a major source of stress. Cooper (1981) outlines a number of stress factors at work (see Figure 1.4).

Working Conditions

There is ample evidence that physical and mental health is adversely affected by unpleasant working conditions, such as excessive noise, too much or too little lighting, high temperatures, and excessive or inconvenient hours.

Work Overload

Quantitative overload refers to having too much to do. You may be competent at your job but time pressure, long hours, unrealistic deadlines, frequent interruptions, and lack of appropriate rest intervals can all elicit a stress reaction.

Qualitative overload means the work is too difficult and the job exceeds the technical and intellectual competence of the individual. The job may involve continuous concentration, high level decision-making and dealing with sophisticated information and the individual may lack the ability to cope with it.

Work Underload

The job fails to provide meaningful psychological stimulation. The individual may feel bored because of the job's repetitive nature, or frustrated because there is no opportunity for self-expression.

Role Ambiguity

The individual has inadequate information about their work role: there is a lack of clarity about work objectives, responsibilities, and colleagues' expectations. Lack of feedback leads to confusion, frustration, helplessness, and stress.

Role Conflict

An individual in a particular work role is torn by conflicting demands, or by doing things that they do not want to do. There may be a difference of view with one's superior, or the job may conflict with personal, social, and family values.

Responsibility

The greater the level of responsibility for people at work, the greater the possibility of stress related reaction.

Relationships at Work

Good relationships are a central factor in individual and organizational health. French and Caplan defined poor relations as those which include 'low trust, low supportiveness, and low interest in listening and trying to deal with problems that confront the organizational member' (French and Caplan 1973). The different relationships to consider include those with superiors, subordinates, and colleagues. Having a supportive social network where problems can be openly expressed and discussed is an important insulator against stress. Problems are exacerbated at highly competitive management levels, where problem sharing can be inhibited for fear of appearing weak and inadequate.

Changes at Work

Any changes which alter psychological, physiological, and behavioural routines are stressful. Promotion will almost certainly

Figure 1.4 Cooper's Job Stress Questionnaire

Could you please circle the number that best reflects the degree to which the particular statement is a source of stress for you at work?

	No stress at all					A great deal of stress
My relationship with my boss	0	1	2	3	4	5
My relationships with my colleagues	0	1	2	3	4	5
My relationships with my subordinates	0	1	2	3	4	5
Workload	0	1	2	3	4	5
Making mistakes	0	1	2	3	4	5
Feeling undervalued	0	1	2	3	4	5
Time pressures and deadlines	0	1	2	3	4	5
Promotion prospects	0	1	2	3	4	5
Rate of pay	0	1	2	3	4	5
Demands of work on my private life	0	1	2	3	4	5
My spouse's attitude towards my work	0	1	2	3	4	5
The amount of travel required by my work	0	1	2	3	4	5
Being relocated	0	1	2	3	4	5
Taking work home	0	1	2	3	4	5
Managing people	0	1	2	3	4	5
Office politics	0	1	2	3	4	5
Lack of power and influence	0	1	2	3	4	5
My beliefs conflicting with those of the company	0	1	2	3	4	5
Lack of consultation and communication in my company	0	1	2	3	4	5
Clarity of my job	0	1	2	3	4	5
Conflict between my work group and others in the organization	0	1	2	3	4	5
Top management does not understand my work-related problems	0	1	2	3	4	5

lead to change in job function, such as increased responsibility and different relationships. Promotion, retirement, and redundancy produce massive changes in routine and a likely reduction in physical, mental, and social activity.

Natural Environment

Numerous factors within the natural or physical environment have been shown to increase stress levels. It seems that the characteristics of certain environments have the effect of arousing the sympathetic nervous system, bringing the stress response into play. Although human beings have an enormous capacity to adjust and adapt to negative unpleasant environments, there do seem to be particular living conditions which consistently produce adverse reactions. These might include living conditions characterized by either excessive overcrowding or isolation, excessive heat, cold, light, or noise, and restrictions which inhibit privacy.

Other factors which we could categorize under the heading of the natural environment might include the type of chemicals we take into our body. This can include the types of chemicals in the air we breath, the water we drink, and the food we eat. A diet high in cholesterol and smoking cigarettes, even passively, have been positively associated with increased risk of a number of physical illnesses. Similarly, lack of physical exercise has been associated with a number of physical disorders, and an increase in physical exercise with positive mental and physical health gains.

THE INDIVIDUAL

Attitudes and Traits

Two areas of research concerning the attitudes and traits of an individual and how they relate to stress will be examined in this section of the model.

Type-A Personality

Certain patterns of behaviour – referred to as Type-A or 'hurry sickness' have actually been shown to contribute to high levels of

Figure 1.5 Type-A Behaviour Questionnaire

Please circle the number which you feel most closely represents your own behaviour:

1 Never Late   5 4 3 2 1 0 1 2 3 4 5   Casual about appointments

2 Not competitive   5 4 3 2 1 0 1 2 3 4 5   Very competitive

3 Anticipates what others are going to say (nods, interrupts, finishes for them)   5 4 3 2 1 0 1 2 3 4 5   Good listener

4 Always rushed   5 4 3 2 1 0 1 2 3 4 5   Never feels rushed (even under pressure)

5 Can wait patiently   5 4 3 2 1 0 1 2 3 4 5   Impatient while waiting

6 Goes all out   5 4 3 2 1 0 1 2 3 4 5   Casual

7 Takes things one at a time   5 4 3 2 1 0 1 2 3 4 5   Tries to do many things at once; thinks what he is about to do next

8 Emphatic in speech (may pound desk)   5 4 3 2 1 0 1 2 3 4 5   Slow, deliberate talker

9 Wants good job recognized by others   5 4 3 2 1 0 1 2 3 4 5   Cares about satisfying himself no matter what others may think

10 Fast (eating, walking, etc.)   5 4 3 2 1 0 1 2 3 4 5   Slow doing things

11 Easy going   5 4 3 2 1 0 1 2 3 4 5   Hard driving

12 Hides feelings   5 4 3 2 1 0 1 2 3 4 5   Expresses feelings

13 Many outside interests   5 4 3 2 1 0 1 2 3 4 5   Few interests outside work

14 Satisfied with job   5 4 3 2 1 0 1 2 3 4 5   Ambitious

Scoring: The questionnaire contains 14 characteristics of Type-A behaviour all rated on a 10 point scale. At one end of each rating scale is the Type-A behaviour; the other end is the Type-B behaviour. High Type-A scores are obtained on the right hand side of the scale for items 2, 5, 7, 11, 13, 14. High Type-A scores are obtained on the left hand side of items 1, 3, 4, 6, 8, 9, 10, 12. To score the questionnaire give yourself 10 points if you score at the end of the scale towards Type-A, working down to 0 points towards the other end of the scale which represents Type-B. The maximum possible score is 140.

stress. Two American cardiologists Friedman and Rosenman (1974) noticed that a great many of the people they saw with coronary heart disease and strokes were of a similar nature, and tended to be rather difficult individuals to rehabilitate, as they had difficulty adjusting to a lifestyle that would assist recuperation.

They therefore carried out a research project involving 3,400 people; results suggested a significant relationship between behavioural patterns and stress related illness. They reported that men with Type-A behaviours in the age group 39–49 years showed a rate of heart disease six times higher than that of men with Type-B behaviour (see Figure 1.5).

Type-A behaviour has four main patterns:

1 *An intense sense of time urgency* – the individual is always in a hurry, trying to get more done in less time.
2 *Inappropriate hostility and aggression* – the individual is excessively competitive and finds it difficult to relax and enjoy fun activities; slight provocation or frustration may trigger off an outburst of hostility.
3 *Multiple behaviour* – the individual engages in two or more things simultaneously at inappropriate times.
4 *Tries to achieve goals without proper planning* – the individual rushes into their work without planning the steps to achieve required goals.

Type-B behaviour, on the other hand, is the exact opposite, the individual characterized by being more relaxed, less hurried, and less inclined to compete.

Type-A behaviour appears to put particular stress on the cardiovascular system, provoking high blood pressure, high heart rate, heart rate variability, and increased risk of heart attacks. According to Friedman and Rosenman (1974) Type-A behaviour leads to excessive discharge of the stress hormones – noradrenalin, adrenalin, and cortisol, and one result is an excess of insulin in the blood stream. This can mean that it takes three or four times longer to get rid of dietary cholesterol after meals. A potential result of this is narrowing of blood vessels, together with increased deposits of clotting elements in the blood.

Cooper (1981) found that the most successful managers tended to be Type-A. However, the cost of that success can be

13

stress related illness. Cooper does not suggest getting rid of Type-A behaviour per se, as it is obviously an adaptive behaviour in certain competitive situations, rather we should learn to manage it appropriately. We will be looking at ways of managing Type-A behaviour in chapter six.

Clinical experience shows that there are other attitudes and traits likely to predispose a person to increased stress. These include: low levels of assertiveness – the person has difficulty expressing personal beliefs, attitudes, and feelings, and has problems limiting demands being made on them by others; and, unrealistically high expectations for self and others – often accompanied by a strong perfectionist streak, wanting to have everything 'just right' and 'under control' – this can lead to high levels of frustration and stress.

The Hardy Personality

Kobasa (1982) developed the concept of the 'hardy personality', carrying out research on people who have managed to stay healthy and happy despite many life changes – such people could be called 'stress resistant'. In a study of 670 managers it was found that there were those who experienced low levels of illness despite high levels of stress, and others who had similar levels of stress but who became ill. It was concluded that psychological resistance to stress seems to be based on the individuals approach to life. Three factors were identified as being important.

First, stress resistant people have a sense of *control* over situations and events in their lives. They have a belief that they can influence the course of events. They accept responsibility for things happening in their lives, rather than seeking explanation in others' actions, or attributing events to fate. They have an internal locus of control rather than an external locus.

Second, there is a feeling of being *committed* and involved in whatever they are doing, whether it be work, family, hobbies, or social situations. Kobasa describes commitment to self as having a sense of purpose and direction, and knowing why that purposeful involvement was chosen.

Third, they have a sense of *challenge*, based on the belief that change rather than stability is the normal course of life. Disruption associated with stressful life events is anticipated, and seen as a positive and creative opportunity for growth rather than a threat to security. They have an ability to be flexible and to deal with ambiguity.

These three attitudes of control, commitment, and challenge were found to be characteristic of the people who managed stress successfully. Alternatively, those who did not cope and experienced stress related problems had a lack of a sense of control over the events in their life, a lack of commitment to themselves, their work, families and social/leisure activities, and they avoided change, seeing it as a threat to their security and as something to be avoided.

Temperament

Claridge (1985) reviewed a large body of research establishing individual differences in physiological arousability or reactivity. Some people get aroused very quickly and take a long time to calm down. Others are slower to be aroused. Measures of arousal would include monitoring heart rate, blood pressure, respiration, muscle tension, perspiration, and endocrine changes. We are all different, but it does seem likely that just as physical characteristics such as height and hair colour are influenced by genetic factors, so is the sensitivity of our autonomic nervous system.

Similarly, just as our overall level of arousal may be influenced by a genetic predisposition, so too are our specific physical responses to stress. Lacey (1967) argues that, although we share a common basic alarm reaction, we all have different idiosyncratic ways of responding to stress. Some people notice stress more in their muscular system, experiencing symptoms such as headaches, others notice it more in their cardiovascular system, experiencing palpitations, while still others might be more vulnerable in their digestive system, the result being feelings of nausea. Some individuals might develop physical reactions such as asthma or coronary heart disease, while their neighbour might have a predisposition or vulnerability to develop a psychotic reaction.

Past Experience and Needs

Undoubtedly childhood experiences have an important deter-mining role in the development of our attitudes, personality,

15

and ways of coping with stress. Types of parental models and the world views they espouse obviously directly influence how a child views situations. On one hand the world can be seen as a playground in which to go out and have fun and where people can be trusted, while at the other extreme parents may convey messages 'the world is a dangerous place', 'always be careful', 'don't trust people, or show people how you feel'. Parents pass on messages to their children, consciously and unconsciously, about how threatening everyday situations are, and how capable they feel their children are of coping with those situations. Consequently some children develop complete confidence and skill in their ability to cope, others less so.

The ability to develop positive early relationships is crucial for the later healthy development of the individual. Bowlby (1969) argues that the formation of early attachments, particularly with parent figures, is crucial to the development of later relationships and for psychological health. In one famous longitudinal study, Valiant (1977) identified individuals who described a 'loveless' relationship with their parents in early childhood. In later life they showed many disadvantages: they didn't 'play' as adults, they were mistrustful and dependent, lacking in friends, and about half of them had mental health problems. Unhappy early relationships can very often lead to similar relationships later in life, affecting the individual's self-esteem and the quantity and quality of social support.

PERCEPTION OF THREAT

Another factor indicated by our stress model is the idea of appraisal or perception of threat. Different people will perceive different events as threatening and stressful. Their perception will depend on their past experience, knowledge, attitudes, beliefs, and values. Take for example the following hypothetical situation. In an examination room a student walks out, half an hour before the end of the exam. From his desk at the back of the class student A thinks to himself, 'Oh no, Charlie Brown's finished already, he's bound to have done well, he's much cleverer than me. I'm nowhere near finished. I've never been any good at taking exams', – he then starts worrying unduly and his performance is affected.

Student B has a completely different perception of the situation. 'Charlie Brown's walking out with a full thirty minutes to go – he must have run out of things to say – he's wasting his time leaving so soon. I've got to try and cram everything I know into this last half hour'. One student judges the event negatively, as threatening, while the other sees it in a positive way and it spurs him on to increased activity.

Some people are 'more aware' than others of the stresses in their lives, their perception is more accurate, they recognize both external demands and they are aware of their own internal demands: in times of stress they naturally make adjustments to their lives. Others are perhaps less aware, or perceptive, or unsightful, and very often cannot 'see the wood for the trees', in times of difficulty. Very often when physical, mental, or behavioural symptoms of stress occur they do not see them as a signal or warning sign to make the relevant adjustments to their lives, but rather misinterpret these symptoms and their meaning in a catastrophic manner. They might then start worrying more about the symptoms, or the results of stress, rather than the primary stresses which caused the symptoms. These factors, such as insight, awareness, and interpretation of symptoms, constitute the individual's perception of threat.

STATE OF STRESS

We can break the effects of stress down into short-term and long-term effects.

The immediate, short-term, alarm reaction is often referred to as 'the fight or flight response'. This term was coined by Cannon (1929) and describes the complex physiological and biochemical reaction that takes place in our bodies in situations of threat or stress. The response is automatic; we have little conscious control over it. It has been a necessary part of our evolutionary survival kit. Without this 'fight or flight' response prehistoric man would not have survived. Many thousands of years ago this response may have been triggered by a threatening wild animal; today that same response can be triggered by a greater variety of situations, from a near miss in a car accident, to pressure at work in the office, to a combination of personal factors, some of which we may not even be aware of. The body's

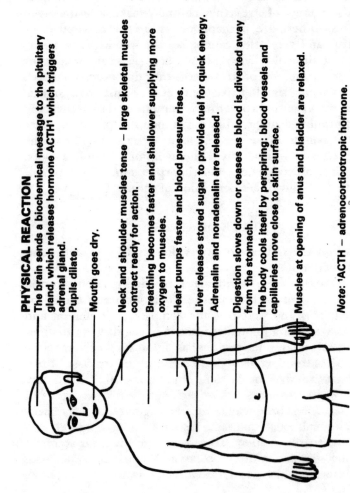

PHYSICAL REACTION

The brain sends a biochemical message to the pituitary gland, which releases hormone ACTH[1] which triggers adrenal gland.

Pupils dilate.

Mouth goes dry.

Neck and shoulder muscles tense – large skeletal muscles contract ready for action.

Breathing becomes faster and shallower supplying more oxygen to muscles.

Heart pumps faster and blood pressure rises.

Liver releases stored sugar to provide fuel for quick energy.

Adrenalin and noradenalin are released.

Digestion slows down or ceases as blood is diverted away from the stomach.

The body cools itself by perspiring: blood vessels and capillaries move close to skin surface.

Muscles at opening of anus and bladder are relaxed.

Note: [1]ACTH – adrenocorticotropic hormone.

SYMPTOM

Headaches, dizziness.

Blurred vision.

Difficulty swallowing.

Aching neck, backache.

Over breathing – chest pains, tingling, palpitations, asthma.

High blood pressure.

Excess sugar in blood, indigestion.

Nausea, indigestion, ulcers.

Excess sweating, blushing.

Frequent urination, diarrhoea.

Figure 1.6 The body's arousal response (alarm reaction)

arousal response, or fight or flight or alarm reaction is detailed in Figure 1.6.

Hans Selye (1946) proposed a three-stage model of stress which he termed the 'General Adaptation Syndrome'. The first stage is the alarm reaction or fight or flight response; the second stage is one of resistance where the body tries to return to a state of equilibrium; and the third stage is that of exhaustion or collapse.

Selye makes the point that stress is a normal part of everyday life and affects all living creatures. He differentiates between two types of stress – eustress and distress. Eustress refers to the level of stress which motivates us to perform well, solve problems, be creative, and grow in confidence. Distress is where our performance deteriorates, our adaptive bodily functioning becomes disrupted, and our response, whether physiological, cognitive, emotional, or behavioural, becomes maladaptive (see Figure 1.7). Selye points out that 'stress becomes dangerous when it is unusually prolonged, comes too often or concentrates on one particular organ of the body'.

COPING STYLE: ADAPTIVE AND MALADAPTIVE COPING STRATEGIES

An important component of the stress model involves the actual responses of the individual to the stresses. Responses can be differentiated into two groups. First, adaptive responses – those actions which help to alleviate the stress and return the system back to a state of equilibrium. Second, maladaptive responses – those actions which serve to exacerbate existing demands and keep the system in a destabilized state.

Adaptive coping is likely to include: recognizing the external stressors and demands, and being aware of personal resources to cope: basically understanding what is going on -- this can include healthy worrying about the situation while taking a problem-solving approach; taking action to reduce external demands – this might include such strategies as making life changes, setting goals, deciding on priorities, time management, delegating, or being more assertive; and taking action to reduce internal demands – this might include taking time to ˙ hysically

19

Figure 1.7   State of stress

PHYSICAL
Increased heart rate, high blood pressure
Hyperventilation
Dizziness, tingling sensations, sweats,
    numbness
Muscle contraction – aches, pains, headaches, shakes
Migraine
Stomach ulcers, nausea
Frequent urination, diarrhoea
Physical illness – asthma, skin rashes,
    cancer, etc.

MENTAL
Difficulty concentrating
Difficulty in making decisions
Impaired memory – forgetfulness
Increased negative self-critical thoughts –
    (Depressive thinking)
Distorted, irrational ideas
Catastrophic thinking – (worrying)

BEHAVIOURAL
Avoidance of anxiety provoking situations
Social withdrawal
Excessive drinking/smoking/drug taking
Difficulty sleeping/early waking
Increased aggression/irritation
Accident-proneness
Manic increase in activity level
Increase in obsessional tendencies
Loss of sexual interest
Alteration in food intake

relax, altering unhelpful thinking patterns, ventilating repressed emotion, and deliberately trying to change behaviour. The results of implementing adaptive coping strategies are that there is an increased likelihood of positive long-term effects. Stresses can be reduced by the individual's own efforts, which produce an increase in confidence, an increase in skill, improved health, and improved resistance to future stresses.

Maladaptive coping strategies are those that are likely to produce further problems: failing to recognize and understand what is happening – this may involve making catastrophic irrational misinterpretations about the situation at hand, or physical symptoms which arise as a result of the situation. These maladaptive worries often lead to a spiralling vicious circle of increased anxiety and increased worry. Maladaptive behavioural responses would include avoidance of situations which produce anxiety, withdrawal from social support, aggression, excessive alcohol consumption, tranquillizer misuse, drug abuse, physical problems, and adoption of the 'sick role'. The long-term effect of these maladaptive strategies is a general loss of confidence in the person's ability to cope on their own, and the development of secondary problems such as, phobic anxiety, tranquillizer dependency, alcoholism, drug addiction, physical illness and depression.

Chapter Two

DIAGNOSTIC CLASSIFICATION AND THEORIES OF ANXIETY

INTRODUCTION

In this chapter we first present the two major systems of diagnostic classification that we use in clinical practice. These divide the diagnosis of anxiety into a number of sub-categories and each of these is explained in detail. Our purpose is to familiarize the reader with clear descriptive criteria of each of these diagnostic groups within the general category of anxiety disorders.

Inevitably, systems of diagnostic classification lag some way behind clinical and academic knowledge. Therefore classification is an evolving process, constantly being refined and reconstrued. Gradually, we are moving away from 'diagnostic' to 'descriptive' criteria, shifting from a medical viewpoint to one which is both humanistic and holistic.

The second half of the chapter deals briefly with four of the major theoretical approaches to the study and treatment of anxiety. The foundations and history of each of these are outlined offering, we hope, a helpful insight rather than a detailed analysis.

DEFINING ANXIETY

The problems of arriving at an exact definition of the term anxiety are immense. Most theorists would agree with Lang (1968) that anxiety is a hypothetical construct. As such it is an assumed notion, having no physical existence, but which may be useful in explaining observable phenomena.

Lang (1969) has offered a three-systems model of anxiety

22

which has assisted greatly in understanding the potential diversity of definitions (see figure 2.1). Anxiety may be construed in terms of *thoughts*, e.g. 'I'm frightened', physical sensations or *feelings*, e.g. increased heart rate, sweating, tension, or *behaviours*, e.g. avoiding a situation or running away. For different individuals their anxiety profile will vary in terms of which system is most pronounced. These three systems are interconnected, having a direct effect on each other.

Figure 2.1 The three-systems model

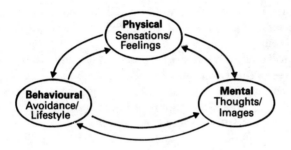

This book takes a holistic view of the clinical problem. Anxiety is defined in the broadest possible sense as a series of physical, cognitive, and behavioural responses to stress.

THE CLINICAL DIAGNOSIS OF ANXIETY

Introduction

There are two widely used systems of diagnostic classification. First, the World Health Organisation's International Classification of Diseases (ICD), which is currently being redrafted, with ICD 10 to be fully introduced in 1993 (Sartorius *et al.* 1988), but currently exists in its ninth revision ICD 9 (1975). Second is the

American Psychiatric Association's Diagnostic and Statistical Manual of Mental Disorders, revised for the third time in 1980 (DSM III) and again in 1987 (DSM III R). Unfortunately, these two diagnostic systems are not identical and there is therefore some difficulty in making international comparison between diagnostic groups. Early drafts of ICD 10 however appear to suggest that the systems are becoming increasingly similar.

Both systems of classification have been based largely on 'medical model' assumptions of psychological abnormality. These suggest that abnormal behaviour is a form of illness and that specific types of behaviour are symptoms which, in combination, form syndromes of mental illness. The emphasis is upon making a primary diagnosis which then suggests a certain aetiology or origin, a specific treatment usually drugs and/or psychotherapy, and a prognosis or predicted course and outcome to the problem.

In its third edition however the DSM has sought to break away in part from this tradition and offers much clearer criteria for each of the diagnostic categories. Likewise early drafts of ICD 10 appear to signal a similar philosophical shift. Definitions are mostly descriptive; theoretical statements are avoided, and aetiology is included only where clearly demonstrable (Gelder, Gath, and Mayou 1983). Both ICD 9 and DSM III systems are presented in relation to anxiety and stress. A greater analysis of the recent revisions of these systems would be premature at this time.

The International Classification of Diseases (ICD 9)

As its name suggests ICD 9 is a classification system for all 'diseases' both physical and psychological. As such 'Mental disorders' form only a small part of the complete volume. Perhaps, because it aims to be widely acceptable in many different countries, it lacks detailed rules of application and though many improvements have been made in the revision from ICD 8 to ICD 9 there is still insufficient information to fully clarify categories of diagnosis.

Anxiety states are listed under the general heading of 'Neurotic Disorders'. Phobic states have a separate sub-heading. Both are presented as follows: (ICD 9 pp. 191–2)

Anxiety States

These include various combinations of physical and mental manifestations of anxiety not attributable to real danger and occuring in attacks or as a persisting state. The anxiety is usually diffuse and may extend to panic, with panic attacks forming part of the clinical picture. Other neurotic features such as obsessional or hysterical symptoms may be present but do not dominate the clinical picture.

Phobic States

These include neurotic states with abnormally intense dread of certain objects or specific situations which would not normally have that effect. If the anxiety tends to spread from a specified situation or object to a wider range of circumstances it becomes akin to, or identical with, anxiety state.

The Diagnostic and Statistical Manual of Mental Disorders (DSM III)

DSM III (1980) offers a greater detail of operational criteria which must be met before specific diagnosis is made. This should lead to significant improvements in the reliability of the diagnostic system as compared to previous editions. The current system also offers a number of specific changes with respect to the diagnosis of anxiety. Formerly anxiety problems were grouped under the general heading 'Neuroses' – defined as conscious or unconscious anxiety. There is no gross distortion of reality, nor is the personality significantly disorganized. DSM III however discards the term 'Neurosis' and groups problems of anxiety under the heading 'Anxiety Disorders'. These are listed, defined, and discussed subsequently:

Phobic Disorders: Agoraphobia with panic attacks
Agoraphobia without panic attacks
Social Phobia
Simple Phobia
Anxiety States: Panic Disorder
Generalized Anxiety Disorder
Obsessive Compulsive Disorder
Post Traumatic Stress Disorder: Acute
Chronic/Delayed
Atypical Anxiety Disorder

Phobic Disorders

A phobia is characterized by an intense fear of an object or situation which is consciously recognized by the person as posing no real danger. The fear is recurrent, intense, and beyond the person's voluntary control. The symptoms include subjective feelings of fear, heightened physiological arousal in the presence of the phobic stimulus, and consequent avoidance behaviours. Since the physiological responses are often themselves very extreme and frightening people with phobias often develop a fear of their own fear response, and their patterns of avoidance can therefore generalize to a large number of situations as a result of this 'fear of fear'.

Simple Phobia

There are a huge number of different types of phobia described in academic and clinical journals. It is estimated that the incidence of phobia in the general population is between 2 and 3 per cent (Marks 1971). The most common specific phobias are of illness or injury, animals, and natural forces such as storms, lightning, etc. These specific fears usually have an early onset (mean age = 5 years) and are often viewed as childhood phobias which have failed to diminish with time (Marks, Gelder, and Edwards 1968).

Agoraphobia with or without Panic Attacks

Other types of phobia suggest a more generalized pattern of fear, often with a number of other associated problems. The most common of these is agoraphobia, first defined in 1871 by Westphal as a fear of public places such as shops and streets, or of public transport. Agoraphobia means literally 'fear of the market place' and is the term used to describe the person's extreme difficulty in leaving a place of safety and entering public places, from which escape may be difficult or help not be available in the case of sudden incapacitation. Two-thirds of agoraphobics are women. The age of onset is typically between 18 and 25 years. Agoraphobics make up from 50–82 per cent of clients seeking therapy for phobic complaints (Marks 1970).

Chambless and Goldstein (1980) have noted that agoraphobics commonly report a variety of symptoms not found with other phobias. Included in these are spontaneous panic attacks, claustrophobia, high levels of general persistent anxiety, experiences of depersonalization, and depression. Agoraphobia can have a very destructive influence upon relationships and within families. Often people close to the client will alter their own life styles to 'fit in with and help' the sufferer. This can often lead to very abnormal patterns of living which may be serving merely to sustain and reinforce the agoraphobia.

As a result of the complex nature of agoraphobia some authors have preferred to describe it as a syndrome (Thorpe and Burns 1983), others have attempted to distinguish between different types of agoraphobia. Goldstein and Chambless (1978) suggest 'complex' and 'simple' agoraphobia as two distinct types. The complex form is beset with a multiplicity of symptoms and behavioural difficulties. With simple agoraphobia the person first experiences difficulties as a result of a physical condition such as hypoglycaemia or drugs; in this case, once the underlying disorder is treated and the fear of fear which has developed is dealt with, the condition improves.

Social Phobia

This refers to anxiety associated with exposure to other people in situations where the individual believes they may be humiliated, criticized, or embarrassed as a result of the scrutiny of others. These fears lead to avoidance of public speaking, public eating, public toilets, strangers, parties, or other social situations.

Clearly many of us would feel apprehensive and anxious if required to speak to a large gathering of people. Beck (1985) however offers a more clear distinction between social phobia and normal anxiety. The socially phobic individual's fears are grossly inaccurate. The individual expects that inept performance in a social situation will be a fatal blow to their social aspirations, their life will be ruined! Should the individual be proved wrong, and the extreme outcome does not occur after a particularly unsettling experience, the individual, none the less, expects disaster next time.

Anxiety States

Marks and Lader (1973) have suggested that anxiety states account for between 6 and 27 per cent of all mental health problems requiring treatment. The condition is more prevalent in women between the ages of 16 and 40 years.

Panic Disorder

This is characterized by episodes of acute anxiety manifested by discrete periods of apprehension or fear. At least four of the following symptoms occur during a panic attack: palpitations, breathlessness, chest pain or discomfort, feelings of unreality, dizziness or unsteadiness, choking or feeling smothered, tingling or numbness in the extremities, hot and cold flushes, sweating, faintness, trembling or shaking, fear of dying, going mad, or losing control, a sudden need to use the toilet.

For a diagnosis of panic disorder DSM III R now requires either four attacks within a four week period, or one or more attacks followed by at least one month of persistent fear of another attack. Sheehan (1982) has stated that panic disorder occurs in between 2–5 per cent of the general population. Brandon (1988) suggests approximately 1 in 50 meet all the criteria for a diagnosis of DSM III panic disorder. Panic attacks may also occur in other anxiety disorders.

Beck (1985) believes that, with training, clients can identify inexplicable physiological sensations, such as faintness or palpitations followed by frightening automatic thoughts, as a prelude to a full blown panic attack. Clark (1986) puts forward a 'cognitive hypothesis' of panic in which he believes that panic attacks arise from a catastrophic misinterpretation of these early bodily sensations. Hibbert (1984) suggested five major themes of catastrophic thoughts in anxious clients: Death or severe illness (including madness), heart attack, failure to cope, extreme social embarrassment, and complete loss of control. Such ideas increase fear and panic, causing the symptoms to worsen and, in turn, intensify the perception of threat. Clark (1986) suggests that these initial bodily sensations occur most commonly in situations previously associated with apprehension and panic. It is possible to argue that the panic attack has already begun to take shape with these initial symptoms and that catastrophic thoughts therefore exacerbate, rather than cause, panic attacks. Either way, it is clear that thinking plays a major role in the aetiology of a panic attack.

Other authors (Ley 1985), have suggested that hyperventilation actually causes panic attacks. This theory is however discounted by Salkovskis (1988) who, reviewing the evidence, suggests that hyperventilation plays an important but probably secondary role in the experience of panic attacks for most clients.

If panic symptoms persist the syndrome may lead to phobic avoidance.

Generalized Anxiety Disorder

Generalized anxiety disorder (GAD) presents as a continuous chronically high level of tension and anxiety of at least one month's duration, in the absence of clear-cut precipitants such as frequent panic attacks (more than three per week) or phobic symptoms.

Such individuals experience pervasive anxiety, with periodic acute attacks that last from a few minutes to several hours, varying from several per day to one or two a month. There is a subjective experience of apprehension, anxiety, and tension associated with behavioural and physiological indices such as motor tremors, rapid eyeblinks, urinary frequency, loss of appetite, concentration difficulties, restlessness, and other symptoms of increased activity of the sympathetic nervous system. Individuals often are unable to say why they are tense and chronically anxious. Because the anxiety is so persistent they are usually handicapped in interpersonal relationships and many other aspects of life (Adams 1980).

Beck (1985) suggests that GAD may result from a series of precipitating psychological factors. First, there may be increased demands upon the individual, who perceives a threat to important values, and a depletion in coping resources. This person typically has greater expectations, increased responsibilities, and an overall increase in energy output. Second, Beck cites that increased threat to life, or to one's domestic situation, can contribute to the development of GAD. For example, a mother might become increasingly anxious about her child who seems to be accident-prone. Third, there may be stressful events which undermine the individual's confidence, for instance: failing exams, rejection by one's partner, or a relatively minor car accident. Individuals with GAD tend to report stressful life events far back into their past and offer a picture of gradually accumulating stress.

Obsessive Compulsive Disorder

This refers to a thought, urge, or overt act characterized as stereotyped, irrational, repetitive, and beyond the voluntary control of the individual. It includes such things as constant checking or washing, over concern with cleanliness, or fear of contamination. Though obsessional and compulsive disorders are associated with other anxiety disorders, they are usually treated as a distinct syndrome by most clinicians. Though much of the information contained in this book applies to this disorder, we do not propose to discuss the specific treatment techniques and complex aetiology related solely to obsessive-compulsive disorder. For further information on this subject readers are referred to Rachman and Hodgson (1980).

Post Traumatic Stress Disorder

Acute, chronic, delayed DSM III describes this condition as the development of characteristic symptoms following a psychologically traumatic event that is generally outside the range of usual human experience.

The characteristic symptoms involve re-experiencing the traumatic event, numbing of responsiveness to, or reduced involvement with, the external world and a variety of autonomic, dysphoric, or cognitive symptoms. Other symptoms of anxiety and depression are common.

The terms acute, chronic, and delayed relate to the onset of the condition and its persistence. Typical events that may lead to post traumatic disorder include serious accidents, involving cars, fires, planes, etc., physical assaults, including rape or other physical violence, and war, especially after battle.

Atypical Anxiety Disorder

This category offers a final diagnostic alternative by excluding all other categories of anxiety disorder for clients presenting with anxiety symptoms.

THEORETICAL APPROACHES TO ANXIETY

This section offers an insight into the four major theoretical perspectives adopted by different clinical practitioners. None of these is totally satisfactory or adequate in explaining the origin and nature of anxiety. However, each has something to offer in furthering the course of science in this field towards a greater understanding of the phenomenon.

Biological Theories of Anxiety

The fact that there is a biological process associated with anxiety is of course undisputed. The question that arises, however, is whether this process is secondary to a primarily psychological mechanism in the underlying aetiology, or whether individuals' differing experiences of anxiety simply reflect their different biochemical make-up and brain function.

In order to understand the complex brain and biochemical processes associated with anxiety it is first necessary to briefly outline some basic neuro-anatomy. The brain may be divided approximately into three areas. The highly developed forebrain area is the centre of intelligence and reasoning. The midbrain, or limbic system, and particularly the amygdala, are associated with emotions. The third area is the hindbrain, the most primitive part of the brain responsible for homeostasis. This area includes the hypothalamus and pituitary gland, and it is these structures that are of particular importance in mediating the biological anxiety and stress responses.

Figure 2.2 The synaptic junction

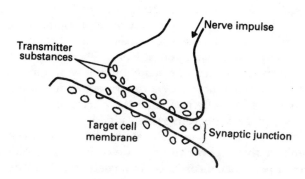

31

Additionally it is important to understand something of the mechanisms of the brain. The basic unit of the human nervous system is the neuron. Sensory information and responses are transmitted by electrical impulses, chemical in nature, which travel along neuronal pathways. These neuronal pathways may have several hundred interconnections which may be to other neurons, to muscles, or to glands. The point at which a neuron interconnnects with other cells is called the synapse (see Figure 2.2). In order for any electrical impulse to be passed on from a neuron the synaptic junction must be bridged by the release of chemical transmitters from the nerve ending into the target cell. These substances then bind to a receptor protein on the external surface of the cell membrane. The effects of the different transmitters on the cell may be excitatory, inhibitory, or modulatory. Figure 2.3 depicts the complex biochemical reactions to stress. As previously stated, in order for these responses to occur neurotransmitter substances at synaptic junctions must innervate the target cells. The biochemical response is therefore mediated by neurotransmitters as well as by hormones.

This dual mechanism becomes clearer when we consider the use of drugs in controlling anxiety states. The benzodiazepine class of tranquillizers, which includes diazepam and lorazepam, mimics the action of GABA (gamma-aminobutyric acid), the brain's most common inhibitory neurotransmitter. By occupying the GABA receptor sites, the benzodiazepines allow the action of three major neurotransmitter substances, serotonin, noradrenalin, and dopamine to become enhanced. This is important because low levels of these substances are linked with the presence of abnormal levels of anxiety or depression. Another form of medication often used for anxiety is the beta-blocker, most commonly propranolol and atenolol. These may be particularly effective in treating the acute physical symptoms, since their effect is to block beta-adrenergic receptors in the heart, and at other sites, thereby inhibiting the effects of adrenaline and other sympathetic nervous system stimuli.

Other theorists have sought to study the possibility of a genetic link in the experience of anxiety. Slater and Shields (1969) cite 41 per cent concordance for anxiety related disorders in monozygotic twins, as compared with 4 per cent for nonidentical twins. Though this may offer some support for

Figure 2.3 Flow diagram depicting the biological anxiety and stress response

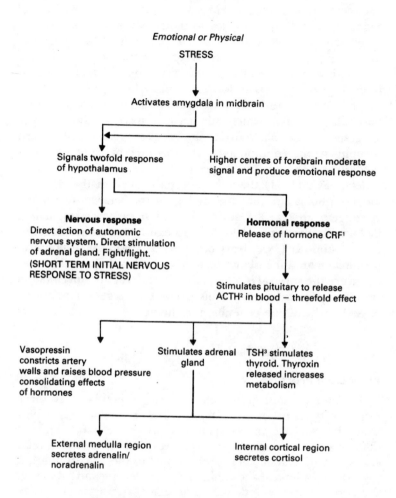

Notes: 1. CRF — corticotrophin-releasing factor
2. ACTH — adrenocorticotropic hormone
3. TSH — thyroid stimulating hormone

bio-medical hypothesis it should be noted that identical twins often experience 'identical environments' as well as genes.

Others, though they would not endorse a solely biomedical model, have offered further evidence for biological involvement. Eysenck (1967) has suggested that individual differences in the experience of anxiety may occur as a result of the inheritance of a particular genetic make-up that predisposes the individual toward high or low 'emotional lability'. This is defined as the tendency to react with greater or lesser intensity to a particular stimulus which might cause distress. Eysenck also suggests that certain individuals are also predisposed toward forming strong conditioned responses thereby combining bio-medical and behavioural theories.

Seligman's (1971) theory of 'preparedness' in the development of phobia also combines biological and behavioural theory. It suggests that as a result of evolutionary processes man is biologically predisposed to develop easily conditioned fears of certain stimuli. These fears occurred as a natural response in primitive man, for instance to spiders, snakes, heights, in order to ensure the survival of the species. Such fears are still common since Seligman believes that this 'preparedness gene' may still be passed on from one generation to the next.

Psychoanalytic Theories of Anxiety

Freudian Theory

In his later writings Freud (1936) distinguished between three different types of anxiety. Objective, or reality, anxiety is possessed by everyone and refers to the capacity to respond to real danger as it occurs in the external world. This anxiety, Freud states, is both rational and proportional to the fear stimulus, it provides an adaptive and rapid means of alerting and preparing the person faced with danger. The other two forms of anxiety are those which cause psychological problems and are known as moral, and neurotic anxiety. In order to fully understand the nature of these it is important to first offer a broad outline of the basis of Freudian theory.

Freud believed that the human personality might be conceptualized as having three basic parts: the id, the ego, and the super-ego. The id is present from birth and is the source of all psychic energy called 'libido'. This energy operates to satisfy primary biological drives including sex, aggression, hunger, thirst, evacuation of the bowels, and sensory needs such as warmth/coolness. The id is entirely hedonistic in nature, seeking immediate gratification without restraint or reference to logic or morality. The ego develops out of the id and acts as a restraining force, taking into account the demands and constraints of reality. The task of the ego is further complicated by having to also take into account the demands of the super-ego. The super-ego may be roughly equated with a 'super conscience' derived from the child's early experiences of reward and punishment, and the moral values of the parents. All human behaviour therefore stems from the complex interplay of these three psychic forces all vying for fulfillment.

Freud suggests that the first experience of anxiety occurs as a result of birth. The infant is dispatched from the security of the womb into a new and unfamiliar situation where he or she perceives suddenly that the needs of the id may not receive immediate gratification. This 'primary anxiety' sets the pattern then for all other experiences of anxiety.

Returning to the second of Freud's three forms of anxiety, moral anxiety refers to a fear of punishment by the super ego for failing to abide by normal standards as a result of actual or potential behaviour directed by the id. Such anxiety takes the form of guilt and shame. The third form, neurotic anxiety, is experienced as a result of the threat of the id to overwhelm the ego, with the consequent socially unacceptable expression of pleasure-seeking or aggressive behaviour. The child has been punished severely for this form of behaviour in the past so, anticipating further punishment, anxiety develops. The ego attempts to repress the impulses of the id, with the super-ego looking on, but in as much as this repression is only partially successful a vague, 'free-floating' anxiety is experienced.

These free-floating anxieties can become attached to things in the real world as the ego attempts to discharge the accumulated tension. The fear is 'projected' into something else which is symbolic of the unconscious conflict and a phobia develops.

These ideas are graphically illustrated by the famous case of 'Little Hans' a 5-year-old boy with a phobia of horses. Briefly, Freud interpreted this fear as symbolic of the child's fear of his father, by whom Hans believed he would be severely punished should his father discover Hans's sexual desires towards his mother. The horse represented his father and then became the phobic object onto which Hans's free-floating anxiety was projected.

Neo-Freudian Theory

These theories developed in the 1930s and 40s, largely as a result of dissatisfaction with what was seen as Freud's over emphasis of the importance of biological impulses, particularly sex, and the threat they posed to the individual. Neo-Freudians regard human personality development as largely a consequence of social influences. They believe that 'primary anxiety' develops not at birth but later, as the child realizes it is dependent upon its parents. The child is dependent not only for gratification of basic physiological needs but also for protection and support. Anxiety is aroused by the actual or potential frustration of these dependency needs. Should the child misbehave the parents might withdraw affection and support. This threat impels the child to conform to the parents' expectations. However, the constant need for the child to repress these impulses creates frustration and then aggression towards the carer. Clearly, if the child was to express this aggression this would lead to rejection and primary anxiety, and it must therefore likewise be suppressed using 'defence mechanisms'.

Secondary anxiety occurs in later life when these deep-seated defence mechanisms, used in early life to suppress primary anxiety, are challenged. For example, an individual may have developed a quiet and unassertive manner as a means of not giving offence and thereby not being rejected. Should a situation develop in later life that calls for assertion this defence against primary anxiety is challenged and a new defence mechanism is required to prevent anxiety developing. This may or may not be possible.

The theory suggests that if the original defences employed against primary anxiety are sound they will not easily be threatened by new situations. If they are weak, or become weakened as a result of prolonged stress, then new defences must be found which will provoke new anxieties, and so on, as neuroses develop.

Behavioural Theories of Anxiety

Watson and Rayner (1920) pioneered the research into a behavioural theory of phobias. They demonstrated that a phobia can be acquired through a process of 'classical conditioning'. This may be best illustrated with their classic case of 'little Albert'. They conducted an experiment whereby every time Albert reached for a white rat to play with, the experimenters struck a steel bar loudly with a hammer. The noise, not surprisingly, produced a fear response in Albert which, after several repetitions of the process, became associated with the white rat and Albert developed a phobia of the rat. The fear response had thus been classically conditioned to the rat by this process of temporal and spatial association where no such fear had previously existed.

Though this experiment is an important landmark in the history of behaviourism it should be noted that other attempts to demonstrate the acquisition of fear by these methods have proved less successful (English 1929). Though classical conditioning may be part of the process, it is clear that life rarely offers repeated exposure of a fear response to an unrelated stimulus in this way and for a fear to develop of this stimulus.

Mowrer (1947) has extended this work by suggesting a two factor theory for the development and maintenance of phobia. Initially fears develop, as stated, through classical conditioning and subsequently the person learns to reduce this fear by avoidance. This second kind of learning is called 'instrumental conditioning' and the response of avoidance is acquired and maintained because it reduces anxiety and is therefore immediately reinforcing.

Seligman's theory of preparedness (Seligman 1971), may also help us to understand how fears become conditioned, since those stimuli for which we are biologically 'prepared' have been shown to condition more rapidly than 'unprepared' stimuli.

Generalized anxiety disorders, it is supposed, develop in a similar manner to phobias. A neutral stimulus is associated with an unpleasant experience and the individual subsequently exhibits a conditioned emotional reaction. However, because it is difficult to specify the phobic cue or because such cues are so pervasive, the person finds it impossible to escape from the fear. Phobia may therefore be thought of as a case of a conditioned avoidance response whereas GAD is a conditioned emotional response.

Friends and family may also rally round to 'help' the anxiety sufferer. This serves to increase social and care giving interactions which may serve as another form of reward for being anxious. As people change their lifestyles to fit in with the problems of the anxious person there is less need to overcome the anxiety itself. Once avoidance becomes established as the means of coping with problems it is used repeatedly. The anxiety may generalize and the person's behavioural repertoire and confidence will quickly diminish.

Cognitive Social Learning Theory (CSL)

This perspective developed from behaviourism and has arisen as a result of dissatisfaction with what was regarded as the rigidity and simplistic notions of pure behaviourism. Bandura (1969) agreed that fear and anxiety are learned but has suggested four possible mechanisms for this learning. First, he states fears may be learned by classical conditioning in exactly the way just described. Second, he suggests that 'vicarious experience' (watching someone else undergo discomfort, punishment, or pain as a consequence of their behaviour) may be important. This process is also termed 'modelling'. Third, 'symbolic instruction' refers to learning through education, reading or being told that certain things are terrifying, painful, or taboo. Fourth, Bandura cites 'symbolic logic' as potentially important in the development of anxiety. A person may infer or deduce something is dangerous. This process may be logical or illogical, for example: sharks swim in the sea, sharks are dangerous, therefore the sea is dangerous.

Cognitive social learning theories therefore attest to the importance of a combination of learning principles together with the role of individual thought and reasoning in the development of anxiety disorders. Another important component to CSL is the idea of self efficacy. Bandura (1977) states that expectations of personal efficacy determine whether, and to what extent, coping behaviours will be initiated. These coping patterns depend upon accurate perception of the situation, prior experience, and the person's confidence of being able to perform the appropriate coping response.

Cognitive Theories of Anxiety

Cognitive theorists believe that it is not events or problems which cause anxiety or stress but rather it is the individual's interpretation of these events that may lead to these problems. Cognitive theories were developed largely as an explanation and treatment approach for depression. More recently they have been applied to the field of anxiety where their emphases and therapeutic implications are equally valid. Though different theorists offer slightly different emphases, cognitive theories in general state that anxiety is maintained by the mistaken or dysfunctional appraisal of a situation leading to perception of danger. In addition to the detailed analysis and restructuring of irrational and faulty patterns of thinking, cognitive therapy methods also employ behavioural target setting as an integral part of the therapeutic process.

Beck (1976) suggests that pathological anxiety stems from the repeated overestimation of danger along one or more of four dimensions:

1 Overestimating the chances of a feared event occurring.
2 Overestimating the severity of the feared event.
3 Underestimating one's own ability to cope.
4 Underestimating the likelihood that someone else will be able to help.

Beck (1985) believes that the anxious person's preoccupation with danger is manifested by the continuous involuntary intrusion of automatic thoughts, either visual images or verbal self statements, whose content involves potential physical or mental harm. Such thoughts may occur so fleetingly that the person is unaware of their occurrence and merely recognizes being in a state of high anxiety.

These thoughts or images are not, however, solely concerned with external situations. The individual is also likely to misinterpret any physical symptoms which may occur in extreme, exaggerated, and catastrophic ways. A mild headache becomes a brain tumour, tightness in the chest a sign of a heart attack, difficulty breathing may be interpreted as imminent death. Such interpretations exacerbate anxiety and therefore increase symptoms.

Beck suggests that anxiety-provoking thoughts are brought

about by one or a combination of four general types of thinking error:

1 Catastrophizing – disaster is the predicted outcome when the anxious person anticipates danger or problems.
2 Exaggerating – minor mistakes or imperfections become absolute failure or fatal flaws.
3 Overgeneralizing – one difficult experience is translated into a law governing the person's entire existence.
4 Ignoring the positive – overlooking all past successes, personal resources, and strengths.

Beck also points out the individual's propensity towards selective scanning during anxious moments. A person who, for example, feels very self-conscious in a queue may notice someone looking at them blankly and interpret this as disapproval, thereby increasing their anxiety. Beck also highlights the capacity of anxious people to relive traumatic events in imagination, whereby those events are reborn with such vividness that they are able to provoke as great an anxiety as the initial event. This may lead to an increase in potential anxiety-evoking stimuli, as more and more things are seen to be associated with the original trauma.

Beck believes that a person's perception of their own vulnerability, defined as an estimate of internal or external dangers over which control is lacking or is insufficient to afford safety, is also central to anxiety disorders. A person minimizes their personal resources, focuses primarily on their weaknesses, magnifies these weaknesses until they become fatal flaws, and then catastrophizes every mistake that they make. These types of thinking errors increase perceived vulnerability and so increase anxiety; confidence is eaten away and avoidance ensues.

Ellis (1962, 1976) extends cognitive theory by proposing that the primary causes of human distress are certain 'core irrational beliefs'. Ellis believes that individuals are happiest when they are able to establish important life goals and purposes and then actively pursue them. Irrational beliefs are defined as those beliefs which stand in the way of the person being able to achieve these goals. Such beliefs are absolutes, expressed in the form of 'have to', 'must', and 'should', setting impossible standards and targets and putting up barriers to successful functioning.

Ellis cites twelve core irrational beliefs which he suggests are the 'primary assumptions' underlying all irrational thoughts:

1 It is a dire necessity for me to be loved by everyone for everything I do.
2 It is horrible when things are not the way I would like them to be.
3 Certain acts are awful or wicked and people who perform such acts should be severely punished.
4 Unhappiness is the result of external events and occurrences which are forced upon us and over which we have no control.
5 If something is, or may be, dangerous or fearsome I should be terribly upset by it.
6 It is easier to avoid life's difficulties than face them.
7 I need something greater or stronger than myself on which to rely.
8 I should be thoroughly competent, intelligent, and achieving in all possible respects.
9 Because something once strongly affected my life, it should indefinitely affect it.
10 I must have certain and perfect control over things.
11 Human happiness can be achieved by inertia and inaction.
12 I have virtually no control over my feelings and I cannot help feeling certain things.

It is easy to see how anxiety may be created in people who believe that they must have certain and perfect control over everything they do, or how social anxiety could stem from believing that everyone they meet must love them and everything they do.

THE THEORETICAL ORIENTATION OF THIS BOOK

The authors' clinical practice is based upon the amalgamation of both a cognitive social learning perspective and a cognitive approach. Blackburn (1986) notes not revolution but evolution in the generally noted shift which began in the 1960s, from pure behaviourism into a more cognitively based clinical practice. She believes that such a shift has been of great value to cognitive therapy since the application of the empiricism of the behavioural tradition has led to much valuable research.

Experimental evidence for a cognitive–behavioural approach in anxiety is now compelling. The importance of cognitive elements in treatment techniques is further highlighted by the findings of Butler and Mathews (1983) who, amongst others, have demonstrated that anxious people experience a selective bias in memory and information processing, which predisposes them towards making anxiety-provoking interpretations through anxious cognitions and images. This occurs pre-attentively and therefore without the anxious person being aware that it is happening.

There is ample evidence that at present pharmacological treatments have little to offer anxiety sufferers in the longer term. Problems of addiction to minor tranquillizers assert the certain need for other psychological and self-help therapies. Some studies (Paul 1966, Smith and Glass 1977) have arguably demonstrated the greater effectiveness of behaviour therapy when compared with other forms of psychotherapy. It is not solely for those reasons, however, that the authors reject these methods as a first line treatment for anxiety disorders. Routine clinical practice does not afford the luxury of time for long-term intervention with the majority of clients. Rather the authors believe that a short-term intervention, involving education, teaching self-help skills, and directive cognitive/behavioural therapy maximizes therapeutic efficiency and effectiveness. This book therefore adopts a cognitive-behavioural paradigm for the modes of clinical practice discussed.

Chapter Three

ASSESSMENT

INTRODUCTION

The first task of a therapist faced with a new client is assessment. A good assessment is important for both therapist and client. The therapist needs to know what the main problems are, what caused them, what maintains them, and what possibilities there are for change. The therapist's objective at the end of the assessment period is to be able to make an approximate formulation of what is going on, and to suggest a provisional treatment plan. From the client's point of view the assessment provides an opportunity to express their difficulties in a structured manner, and make links between specific problems and various areas of their life, both past and present. At the end of the assessment the client will be reassured that the problem is understandable, and that there is 'light at the end of the tunnel', in terms of a provisional treatment plan.

The ability to carry out a good assessment requires the combination of a number of personal skills, and the active use of a large body of knowledge. The skilled interviewer has to establish a fine balance between being receptive – allowing the client to relax and talk freely – and being in control – so that the client is guided into talking about fruitful areas, and also that the interview is closed on time.

THEORETICAL APPROACH TO ASSESSMENT

The assessment presented in this chapter is based largely on a cognitive–behavioural model, but encompassing both 'psychodynamic' and 'systemic' approaches. Lazarus (1976) coined the phrase multi-modal assessment, encouraging the interviewer to look at different aspects of the presenting problem. These form the memorable mnemonic BASIC ID – Behaviour, Affect, Sensation, Ideation, Cognition, Interpersonal, and Drugs. Along similar lines, Lang (1969) again broke the presenting anxiety problem down, using three interconnected, but separate systems: physical sensations or feelings, thoughts and images, and behaviour. Lang's three-system model of anxiety plays a central part in both our assessment and treatment programme. The original overwhelming mass of stress or anxiety is broken down into smaller, interconnected parts, providing the client with greater understanding of the processes involved, and greater control over individual components of their anxiety.

This chapter will describe a structured, time-limited, assessment interview, and later examine a number of helpful questionnaires and inventories. For a more detailed description of cognitive–behavioural assessment strategies see Kendall and Hollon (1981).

A three-sided assessment sheet, not printed to scale, is reproduced in Figure 3.1, and offers a guideline to the structure of the interview. This form, printed on three sides of A4 paper, is a useful way of recording information elicited during the interview. The assessment sheet corresponds to the three main sections of the interview, eliciting presenting problems, background information, and formulation and treatment plan.

THE STRUCTURED ASSESSMENT INTERVIEW

Introducing the session

After the therapist has introduced him/herself, explaining something about their profession, and the actual referral process, they might continue by explaining how the first session will proceed.

Therapist: 'What we will do in this first session is an assessment of exactly what's going on: first we will look at the problems at the moment; second we will look at background factors such as your family and personal history; and third we will try to pull it all together and formulate what is going on, and then decide on what the best course of action is.

Figure 3.1 Assessment sheets

PAGE 1

ASSESSMENT FORM: NAME

DATE

PRESENTING PROBLEMS: (What, where, when, how long, antecedents, consequences)

Physical symptoms	Thoughts, images
Precipitating stresses	Behaviour-avoidance
Maintaining factors	First, worst, last	Referral medication

PAGE 2

BACKGROUND FACTORS:

FAMILY – Age, occupation, personality relationship

FATHER
MOTHER
OTHERS
SIBLINGS

PERSONAL HISTORY – Childhood, school, work, relationships

PRESENT SITUATION – Friends, interests, habits, hobbies

PAGE 3

CHANGES CLIENT WOULD LIKE TO MAKE:

FORMULATION:

TREATMENT PLAN:

'So let's look at the current problems first – what is happening at the moment? What I'd like you to do, is to try and put into words, what the main problems are at the moment, when they occur, where they occur, and how long they've been going on for'.

The client will then talk about what is troubling them. This will probably come out as a mixture of physical symptoms, environmental, and individual stresses. The therapist should let the client talk for a while, giving them the opportunity to relax. Then, the therapist can try to shape what has been said by introducing the notion that anxiety is made up of three separate components.

Physical Symptoms

Therapist: 'You say you feel awful at times; let's look at that and try and break it down into the physical sensations you feel, the thoughts you have, and how it effects your behaviour. What kind of physical symptoms do you experience?'

The client may well give a list of physical symptoms, such as palpitations, hot flushes, nausea, headaches, dizziness, other pains, breathlessness. These should be carefully recorded. It is helpful at this stage to establish whether the client has panic attacks, and whether there is any degree of hyperventilation.

Thoughts (Mental Symptoms)

Therapist: 'Now let's look at the thoughts which go with these symptoms. When these symptoms occur what thoughts run through your mind? ... What do you think is happening to you? ... What is your fantasy? ...'

Here the therapist is looking for 'catastrophic thoughts'. These are thoughts that exaggerate and misinterpret the significance of symptoms and generate further physiological arousal and anxiety. The client may say, 'My heart was beating so fast I thought I was going to have a heart attack', or, 'I can't cope any more', or, 'I think I'm going to end up in a mental hospital'.

This network of 'catastrophic thoughts' is the basis for secondary anxiety, in other words, 'worry about anxiety'. The client worries about having a panic attack, or feeling sick, or not coping or any of a number of catastrophic consequences. This worry increases physiological arousal, making it more likely that physical symptoms will occur in the future; an upwardly spiralling vicious circle soon gets established. It is important to establish how much the client worries about the physical symptoms compared to the primary stresses which cause the symptoms. Sometimes the client's main worry is the physical symptoms, and the original stresses which causes those symptoms are no longer an important issue. The original stress may have disappeared but the anxiety symptoms are maintained by a vicious circle of catastrophic thoughts and maladaptive behaviour.

The therapist may have to prompt the client to elicit these thoughts, as very often the client is not aware of them. Once the therapist has extracted one thought they can find out the one behind it. One by one the client's chains of increasingly irrational thoughts can be extracted rather like a magician pulling a series of connected handkerchiefs out of a pocket. Discovering these chains or networks of negative irrational thoughts is the basis of cognitive therapy. When these thoughts are elicited the therapist should reassure the client that a great many people who have worrying physical symptoms have similar catastrophic thoughts which are usually unfounded.

If the client is not specifically worried about the symptoms, the therapist should find out what he is worried about, and pursue that to the end of the chain. Very often there will be an exagerrated catastrophic image or fantasy at the back of the client's mind (i.e., 'I'm unlovable and will never be able to have a good relationship', or, 'I'm not as good as anybody else', or, 'This job is too difficult for me, I can't cope with it', etc.) All these self-statements are based on 'all or nothing', irrational, catastrophic interpretations of reality. It is this style of thinking which plays a large part in producing symptoms of stress.

Behavioural Symptoms

Therapist: 'Now we have looked at the physical symptoms and the thoughts that accompany them, let's now look at how anxiety effects your behaviour. How do you think your behaviour has changed recently? ... More specifically, do you find yourself avoiding things you used to do?'

47

Clients with agoraphobic tendencies will describe a number of situations that they avoid because of the common element of entrapment and distance from a place of safety, i.e. crowded shops, lifts, queues, buses, trains, distance from home, etc. After looking for agoraphobic avoidance, the therapist should look for social avoidance. For example, since being under stress the client may have started to avoid business or social situations. The therapist should look also for any avoidance of previously enjoyed recreational hobbies such as squash, golf, or sailing. Very often when people are under stress these very important relaxing activities get squeezed out of the weekly timetable.

The therapist should look also for other maladaptive behavioural coping strategies such as increasing consumption of alcohol, drugs, cigarettes, food, or prescribed medication. Here, the therapist is looking for maladaptive coping strategies which can be altered at a later date in homework assignments. The client will then deliberately and gradually, confront, or alter these difficult situations and cope with the anxiety they create, using newly acquired coping skills. Anxiety management training is about helping clients to understand what is going on, then teaching them skills to cope with anxiety, then encouraging them to put themselves deliberately into situations which create anxiety but with which they cope successfully. The therapist is therefore looking for situations which create anxiety in the client.

Examples of 'First', 'Worst', and 'Last' Episodes of Anxiety

Therapist: 'Now we have some idea of the physical, mental, and behavioural dimensions of your symptoms, let's now look at how it all started. I'd like you to tell me about the first time you were really aware of these symptoms, then the worst episode you can remember, and then the last. . . . What situations come to mind?'
Very often people are almost haunted by one particular experience and they think to themselves, 'Oh no, I couldn't stand it if it happened like that again'.

The first frightening experience of a panic attack, coming 'out of the blue' can, very often, also be their worst experience. It is the memory of this event which generates further anxiety. The therapist should encourage the client to describe these experiences in terms of the three-systems model (physical, mental, behavioural), then ask them to describe what was going on in their life at the time, and what sort of stresses they were under. Very often, with the benefit of hindsight, people can look back on their lives and identify stressful times more easily than identifying the present stresses that may surround them.

Precipitating Stresses

Therapist: 'What sorts of stresses have you been under recently? Think of a stress as being any change in your life, or an increase in the demands being made on you.'

Some clients will identify obvious external factors, such as changes at work, home, or in their personal life. Other clients appear less aware of these changes, and often don't equate change as being stressful. Gentle prompting and reassurance is often needed.

Therapist: 'One of the main features of people under stress is that very often they "can't see the wood for the trees". When it's all happening around you it's difficult to step back and get a clear perspective. Let's look at it from a different angle; if you could change anything about your life, what would you change?'

If no obvious precipitating stressors are elicited, the therapist should leave it and return to this area when they know more about the client's past history, pre-morbid personality, and present situation.

Maintaining Factors

Therapist: 'Sometimes these types of difficulties can be affected by how other people respond to them. How have your family and friends reacted to your recent difficulties?'

The social network the client is enmeshed in can be vitally important in maintaining the problems; particularly in the case of phobic anxiety. A classic example is the agoraphobic house-wife whose husband is, 'really wonderful, very sympathetic and understanding ... he does everything for me ... he comes around all the shops with me and drives me wherever I want to go'. In this case the husband's behaviour might be positively reinforcing the wife's avoidance behaviour. His attention and company are pleasant consequences, and are likely to strengthen the wife's avoidance response. In some situations the presenting problem may have the function of balancing a particular relationship, i.e. the 'well husband' may feel slightly inadequate but when his wife takes on the 'sick dependent role', he starts to feel more adequate, needed and important. He feels good when she needs him. The couple may not be aware of this process and this issue may need to be handled carefully during the course of therapy.

Family Background

Therapist: 'OK, we have looked at your current difficulties, let's now look at some background information [turns page of assessment sheet]. What I'd like you to do is to describe briefly each of the members of your family – the family you grew up in. Just give a few details about age, occupation, their personality, and your relationship with them. Anything that comes into your head. Let's start with your father'.

This information is important in understanding the circumstances and influences on the development of the client's personality and belief systems. Although these familial influences are unlikely to be the primary focus of the intervention, they are important points of reference, helping both the therapist and client make sense of the presenting problems.

There are a number of important factors to look out for. How have the parents acted as role models? What messages have parents given to the child about itself and the world the child lives in? For example, 'the world is a dangerous place, there is lots to worry about', or, 'children should be seen and not heard', or, 'you are not as important as other people'. What type of relationship did those parents offer the child? Was the child allowed to express a wide and deep range of emotion, or was the expression of particular feelings taboo? Did the child have the opportunity to learn to play, relax, and enjoy itself? The therapist should note how other siblings within the family have faired and whether they have had any stress related problems.

Personal History

Therapist: 'Now I'd like you to run through your personal history, saying something about your childhood, school, work, and relationships ... anything that comes to mind.'

It is important to try to see the client's present difficulties in the context of their life history. Are the present problems unusual or has the client a long history of similar difficulties? The issues to investigate might include whether the client has viewed previous difficulties as challenges or disasters, their ability to establish and maintain relationships, their tendency to worry, and their inclination to avoid rather than confront anxiety provoking situations. This information helps paint a picture of the client's pre-morbid personality. Spielberger (1972) made an important differentiation between 'trait anxiety' and 'state anxiety'. The former suggests a long-standing enduring personality trait or outlook – whether the world is generally viewed as a frightening place and whether the client is prone to anxiety state. The term 'state anxiety' refers to a temporary subjective feeling of tension and apprehension. Obviously people who are merely going through a bad patch (anxiety state) are easier to assist in the process of change, because they have greater resources, than individuals who have always been anxious (anxiety trait).

Present Situation

Therapist: 'OK, now let's come up-to-date and look at your present situation. How do you like to spend your spare time? ... Would you say that you have many people you could talk to; people you would call friends?'

Are there any activities or hobbies that the client would use as distractor to release energy and tension? Very often when individuals are under stress the very activities that they should endeavour to keep in their weekly timetable get squeezed out or avoided. The interviewer is looking for a relapsed sport or hobby which can be restarted and used as behavioural tasks in homework assignments. The social needs of the client can also be an important part of the jigsaw. The client may have needs for a high level of social contact, which for various reasons are not being met, or, vice versa, they may have the need to spend more time alone which is not being met.

Changes the Client Wants to Make

Therapist: 'Everybody who comes here to see a psychologist has different expectations. Some people expect to see a Sigmund Freud-like figure and to lie down on a couch. What were your expectations? And specifically what sort of things would you like to change about yourself?'

Finding out the expectations of clients is important in assessing how readily they will take to an educational self-help approach. If they are looking for an easy, magical cure – either hypnosis or a special pill – they will be disappointed. If they are looking for the special therapist to 'cure' them, then, also they will be disappointed. The therapist should emphasize that encouragement, information, and direction can be offered, but ultimately the client will have to learn to change things for him/herself.

The most important question is, 'What does the client want to do – specifically, what changes do they want to make?' The importance of asking this question is two fold. First, the therapist is placing responsibility for change firmly on the client's shoulders, reinforcing the notion that people help themselves. Second, the therapist is asking the client to be specific and realistic, so that the therapist has goals to aim for. The therapist should challenge any vague and woolly replies, such as 'I just want to get better' or, 'I'd like to be a better person'. They should encourage the client to commit him/herself to something specific, i.e., 'I'd like to stop having panic attacks', or 'I'd like to be able to catch the train up to London', or, 'I'd like to understand and cope more effectively with my anxiety symptoms', or, 'I'd like to be more relaxed giving presentations at work'.

It can also be enlightening to ask about the circumstances of the original referral. Was it the client's idea or the GP's? This information can often be important for assessing the client's motivation: they may only be there to please their doctor.

Formulation and Treatment Plan

At the end of the first session the therapist will try to pull all the information together and make sense out of what has been said, feeding back to the client some explanation and treatment plan. This is perhaps the most difficult part of the assessment but becomes easier with increased knowledge and experience. The therapist cannot expect to be able to do it easily and accurately straightaway or every time. The therapist should always err on the side of caution; the hypotheses set up are merely shrewd guesses. We can all be wrong. The following example is a hypothetical formulation and treatment plan.

Therapist: 'So let's try to pull it all together. Over the last eighteen months there have been a number of major changes in your life. You've moved house and now live in an area away from your family and old friends. You've changed jobs, moving to a position of greater responsibility, where a lot of people are making demands on your time and expertise. Work load has increased and you've found it difficult to say "no", or to delegate. . . . Is that right? . . . Then, out of the blue, at a business meeting you had a "panic attack", characterized by hyperventilation and palpitations. You felt dizzy and extremely frightened, imagining all sorts of frightening thoughts. The main thoughts that worried you were that you were either having a heart attack or that you'd pass out in front of your colleagues. . . . That must have been really worrying? . . . You then left that meeting, rather hurriedly, before it ended, in a very anxious state. That evening you visited your GP who told you to take it easy and prescribed a course of tranquillizers. After that it sounds like you were then constantly on the look out for further physical symptoms. This over-vigilance or sensitization meant that you were noticing all sorts of minor physical symptoms you would have normally ignored. . . . A few further panic attacks increased your worry that something was seriously wrong . . . From what you say it sounds as if, from then on, you started to avoid large business meetings deliberately, and to avoid dining in the staff canteen. Your mood went down and you found yourself avoiding meeting friends and playing golf. . . . It would appear that this vicious circle of anxiety, or anxiety about anxiety, spiralled upwards. For the last month you have been signed off sick from work, which has meant that your confidence in your ability to cope has further diminished. Would that be a fair summary of what you told me? ...'

'It's a familiar story – a number of identifiable stresses or life events acting on a perhaps vulnerable personality, resulting in frightening symptoms, which are misinterpreted and become a major source of worry in themselves. I say that perhaps you might be a "vulnerable" person, because you say that you've always been "a bit of a worrier", finding it difficult to relax; and your mother also appears to have been an anxious person. You also come across as a bit of a perfectionist, having to do everying perfectly and finding it difficult to delegate, or say "no". ... Would that be a fair comment? ...'

'So what can we do? First we can try to dismantle the secondary problem of getting anxious about anxiety, or worry- ing about symptoms. This can be achieved by understanding more about what is going on. Once you know what is happening it becomes much less frightening. Understanding the processes involved, the stages in the development of your difficulties, is the first step. This might involve learning about exactly what a panic attack is. We will then look at some coping strategies such as muscle relaxation, breathing exercises, distraction techniques, and positive self-talk, which will help you to develop a sense of control over your symptoms. Once you feel more able to control symptoms we can set about confronting situations that you have been avoiding, such as meeting people and going to work. It might then be a good time to look at the original sources of stress which created these symptoms in the first place. It sounds like you may benefit from looking at some time management strategies for coping more effectively at work, and also looking at how you could be more assertive in order to limit the demands colleagues make on you. How does that sound?'

The client, it is hoped, will feel reassured at the end of the assessment interview. The message the therapist is conveying is that 'your problem is understandable, it is not strange or abnormal, and there is a recognized course of treatment'. The therapist is offering 'light at the end of the tunnel', something to aim for. The client may be offered a number of options at the end of the session. These might include a number of individual sessions, or a place in an anxiety management group, or even perhaps no further involvement. If individual sessions are the chosen option, the therapist may give the client a number of handouts to read before the next session and a self-monitoring sheet to record incidents of anxiety.

SELF-MONITORING

Self-monitoring of identified behaviours the client would like to change is both part of the assessment procedure and part of the treatment package. The client is given a number of record forms and is instructed to make an entry whenever they notice an inappropriate increase in anxiety. They record the time, place, activating situation, their physical symptoms and thoughts. They are also encouraged to rate their anxiety on a scale of 0–100, and to describe how they coped with the anxiety (see Figure 3.2).

From an assessment point of view this information establishes a baseline record of frequency of panic attacks or other physical symptoms. It also helps the therapist identify antecedents, prominent physical symptoms, and catastrophic thoughts.

Self-monitoring also helps the client to see their difficulty in a different way. They are encouraged to try and take a few steps back and be a little more objective with themselves. This helps the client begin to redefine the problem in a structured cognitive-behavioural way, rather than in their catastrophic, idiosyncratic way. The information gained from the self-monitoring sheets is then used in the next session as a basis for discussion. Research indicates that behaviour may be altered by the very fact that it is being monitored. This phenomenon of 'reactivity' is well accepted; desirable behaviours often increase and undesirable behaviours generally decrease when they are monitored.

THE USES OF QUESTIONNAIRES AND INVENTORIES

Assessment questionnaires and inventories can be useful to both therapist and client for a number of reasons. First, they help map out a profile of the client's problems. In our case this is in terms of mood disturbance, physical symptoms, catastrophic thoughts, avoidance behaviour, and general effects on specific areas of everyday life. Once this map has been plotted, interventions can be specifically targeted at particular areas. Second,

Figure 3.2 Diary record sheet

Please make an entry whenever you notice a definite increase in anxiety.

Name ....

Date/ time	Anxiety 0–100	Activity: What you were doing at the time.	Frightening feelings/thoughts. Did you notice any bodily feelings, or thoughts?	Coping method: Did you try any?	Rate anxiety after coping. 0–100

quantifiable psychometric information can provide a useful baseline from which to work, and from which progress can be measured. This informs the therapist whether their intervention is effective, and enables them to make comparisons between different types of therapy. Having a tangible record of progress can also act as positive feedback and reinforcement for the client. Third, quantifiable data is the cornerstone of applied clinical research. Attempting to shape therapeutic interventions in a form that allows a research project to develop may add a rewarding dimension to clinical work, and often stimulates more academic interest.

A USEFUL BATTERY OF ANXIETY QUESTIONNAIRES

It is our practice to send out a small booklet of self-assessment questionnaires to any client referred to the department with anxiety related problems. This collection of questionnaires takes approximately ten to fifteen minutes to complete and can be used alongside the assessment interview. Very often, during the assessment interview, the therapist might glance at the client's completed inventories and adapt their line of questioning, or confirm a particular response.

The majority of the following questionnaires have been used by other authors for research purposes, so that they are accompanied by some normative data.

For the first part of the battery (Section 1) we use the Hospital Anxiety and Depression Scale (Zigmond and Snaith 1983) (See Figure 3.3). This is a fourteen-item, screening inventory, designed to detect alterations in mood, specifically states of anxiety and depression. There are seven questions relating to anxiety symptoms, (questions 1, 4, 5, 8, 9, 12, and 13) and seven questions relating to symptoms of depression, (questions 2, 3, 6, 7, 10, 11, and 14). The questionnaire is scored on a four-point scale (0, 1, 2, 3). The authors suggest a cut-off point of eleven, scores greater than this indicating clinical significance. High scores on the depression scale suggest that treatment other than anxiety management might also be considered.

Section 2 is a physical symptom inventory (figure 3.4) designed by the authors. Responses are scored on a four-point scale (0, 1, 2, 3).

Figure 3.3 Hospital Anxiety and Depression Scale

SECTION 1

NAME: **DATE:**   **AGE:**

This section is designed to help identify how you feel. Read each item and place
a tick in the box opposite the reply which comes closest to how you have been
feeling in the past few weeks. Don't take too long over your replies: your
immediate reaction to each item will probably be more accurate than a long
thought out response.

Tick only one box in each section

(1) I feel tense or 'wound up':
    Most of the time ....
    A lot of the time ....
    Time to time, Occasionally ......
    Not at all ....

(2) I feel as if I am slowed down:
    Nearly all the time ....
    Very often....................
    Sometimes ....
    Not at all ....

(3) I still enjoy the things I used to
    enjoy:
    Definitely as much.............
    Not quite so much ....
    Only a little ....
    Hardly at all ....

(4) I get a sort of frightened feeling like
    'butterflies' in the stomach:
    Not at all ....
    Occasionally ....
    Quite often ....
    Very often....................

(5) I get a sort of frightened feeling
    as if something awful is about to
    happen:
    Very definitely and quite badly ..
    Yes, but not too badly ....
    A little, but it doesn't worry me ...
    Not at all ....

(6) I have lost interest in my
    appearance:
    Definitely ....
    I don't take so much care as I should
    I may not take quite as much care
    I take just as much care as ever

(7) I can laugh and see the funny side
    of things:
    As much as I always could ......
    Not quite so much now ....
    Definitely not so much now .....
    Not at all ....

(8) I feel restless as if I have to be
    on the move:
    Very much indeed ....
    Quite a lot ....
    Not very much ....
    Not at all ....

(9) Worrying thoughts go through my
    mind:
    A great deal of the time ....
    A lot of the time ....
    From time to time but not too often ..
    Only occasionally ....

(10) I look forward with enjoyment to
    things:
    As much as ever I did ....
    Rather less than I used to ......
    Definitely less than I used to ....
    Hardly at all ....

(11) I feel cheerful:
    Not at all ....
    Not often.....................
    Sometimes....................
    Most of the time ....

(12) I get sudden feelings of panic:
    Very often indeed ....
    Quite often ....
    Not very often ....
    Not at all ....

(13) I can sit at ease and feel relaxed:
    Definitely ....
    Usually ....
    Not often.....................
    Not at all ....

(14) I can enjoy a good book or radio or
    TV programme:
    Often........................
    Sometimes....................
    Not often.....................
    Very seldom ....

58

Figure 3.4 Physical Symptoms Inventory

SECTION 2

Please tick the appropriate choice as to how often you have experienced the following physical symptoms during the last two weeks.

	Not at all	Occasion-ally	Often	Most of the time
1 Palpitations				
2 Breathlessness/rapid breathing				
3 Chest pains or discomfort				
4 Choking or smothering sensation				
5 Dizziness or feeling unsteady				
6 Tingling or numbness				
7 Hot and/or cold flushes				
8 Sweating				
9 Fainting				
10 Trembling or shaking				
11 Feeling sick				
12 Upset stomach/diarrhoea				
13 Headaches/migraine				
14 Dry mouth: difficulty swallowing				
15 Feeling of unreality				
16 Tension in jaw/neck/shoulders				
17 Jelly legs				
18 Any other physical symptoms				

Figure 3.5 Cognitive Anxiety Questionnaire

SECTION 3

This section is about your THOUGHTS and worries about your anxiety.
Please tick the appropriate choice as to how often you have experienced the following thoughts during the last two weeks.

	Not at all	Occasion- ally	Often	Most of the time
1 'I'm going to have a heart attack'				
2 'I'm going to faint'				
3 'I'm going to look a fool'				
4 'I'm walking off balance'				
5 'People are looking at me'				
6 'I'm going to go mad'				
7 'I'm going to be too anxious to speak properly				
8 'I'm not going to be able to cope'				
9 'I'm going to have a panic attack'				
10 'I'm going to choke'				
11 'Why do other people cope better than I do?'				
12 'I can't face up to this because I will not be able to do it'				
13 Any other worrying thoughts				

Figure 3.6 The Fear Inventory (Behavioural Symptoms Questionnaire)

SECTION 4

Choose a number from the scale below to show how much you would avoid each of the situations listed below because of fear or other unpleasant feelings. Then write the number you chose in the box opposite each situation.

0	1	2	3	4	5	6	7	8

Would not avoid it		Slightly avoid it		Definitely avoid it		Markedly avoid it		Always avoid it

1 Injections or minor surgery

2 Eating or drinking with other people

3 Hospitals

4 Travelling alone by bus or coach

5 Walking alone in busy streets

6 Being watched or stared at

7 Going into crowded shops

8 Talking to people in authority

9 Sight of blood

10 Being criticized

11 Going alone far from home

12 Thought of injury or illness

13 Speaking or acting to an audience

14 Large open spaces

15 Going to the dentist

16 Other situations (describe)

leave blank

Ag + Bl + Soc = Total

Figure 3.7 Effects on Life Inventory

SECTION 5

Could you describe what effect your complaints have had in the following areas?
Please circle the appropriate number.

   (i)   *WORK*   Because of my problems my work is impaired:

0	1	2	3	4	5	6	7	8

| Not at all | | Slightly | | Definitely | | Markedly | | Very severely
I cannot work |

   (ii)   *HOME MANAGEMENT*   (Cleaning, tidying, shopping, cooking, looking after children, paying bills)

Because of my problems my home management is impaired:

0	1	2	3	4	5	6	7	8

| Not at all | | Slightly | | Definitely | | Markedly | | Very severely
I cannot do it |

   (iii)   *SOCIAL LEISURE ACTIVITIES*   (with other people, e.g. parties, pubs, clubs, outings, visits, dating, home entertainment)

Because of my problems my social leisure is impaired:

0	1	2	3	4	5	6	7	8

| Not at all | | Slightly | | Definitely | | Markedly | | Very severely
I never do these |

   (iv)   *PRIVATE LEISURE ACTIVITIES*   (done alone, e.g. reading, gardening, collecting, sewing, walking alone)

Because of my problems my private leisure is impaired:

0	1	2	3	4	5	6	7	8

| Not at all | | Slightly | | Definitely | | Markedly | | Very severely
I never do them |

   (v)   *FAMILY LIFE*   (relations with parents, brothers and sisters, playing with children, going out with spouse and family, visits to in-laws, doing leisure activities with spouse)

Because of my problem my family life is impaired:

0	1	2	3	4	5	6	7	8

| Not at all | | Slightly | | Definitely | | Markedly | | Very severely
I never do these |

   (vi)   *INTIMATE RELATIONSHIPS*   (giving affection, hugging, kissing, receiving affection, sexual interest, sexual relations)

Because of my problem my intimate relationships are impaired:

0	1	2	3	4	5	6	7	8

| Not at all | | Slightly | | Definitely | | Markedly | | Very severely
I never do these |

Section 3 (Figure 3.5) is the 'Cognitive Anxiety Questionnaire', described by Lindsay *et al.* (1987), which is a list of the twelve most commonly elicited thoughts associated with feelings of anxiety, drawn from a sample of anxious clients. Responses are scored on a four-point scale (0, 1, 2, 3).

Section 4 (Figure 3.6) is the short form of 'The Fear Questionnaire' (Marks and Mathews 1979), a useful measure of avoidance behaviour in phobic clients. A total phobic score can be computed, or individual subscales can be computed, agoraphobia (Questions 4, 5, 7, 11, and 14), blood and injury phobias (questions 1, 3, 9, 12, and 15), and social phobia (questions 2, 6, 8, 10, and 13).

Section 5 contains the 'Effects On Life Inventory' (Figure 3.7), devised by Mathews (1982, unpublished manuscript). This inventory identifies exactly which areas of the client's life are most disrupted by their problems.

Chapter Four

ANXIETY AND STRESS – THE PROCESS OF EDUCATION

INTRODUCTION

One of the central elements to any course of anxiety management training is helping the client to achieve a greater understanding of the origins, course and nature of the anxiety symptoms. This information is complex and therefore it must be imparted in a language and form that the client can not only understand but also is able to remember.

A strategy for this process of education is presented. It relies heavily on tangible examples, metaphor, and analogy in an attempt to simplify the experience of, and knowledge about, stress and anxiety.

THE PROCESS OF EDUCATION

Some Stress and Anxiety is Normal and Necessary

A certain amount of anxiety is both normal and necessary to perform any task properly. For instance it is unlikely that we will cross a road safely if we are not mildly anxious. However, too much or little anxiety will always affect any performance in a detrimental way. Let us take a particular example. Suppose you are required to perform the simple task of placing each of a pile of twenty counters into a jam jar, picking up one counter at a time and dropping it into the jar. Now let us consider three different conditions each representing a different degree of anxiety within the same task. First you are told that you can take as long as you like to put the counters in the jar. Don't worry, no one is going to ever check up on you, you are only doing it for yourself. These demands create very low anxiety; you may well think to yourself, 'Who cares how quickly I do it.' Thus your performance may well be careless and slow. Second let us suppose that you are told that for every counter that you place in the jar within thirty seconds you will receive a pound coin. Under these conditions your anxiety will be greater, as you are keen to earn as much money as possible in the time allowed. Therefore your task performance is likely to be very fast and efficient. Third, you are told that for every counter that you fail to get into the jar within thirty seconds you will have a finger chopped off. Clearly this condition will create very high levels of anxiety and in your haste you will be likely to fumble the counters or miss the jar altogether.

Figure 4.1 The relationship between anxiety and performance

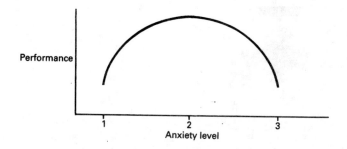

This information is simplified in Figure 4.1. Performance on any task therefore, from playing tennis, to taking exams, to going to work, will be impaired if anxiety is too high or too low, but somewhere between these lies the ideal degree of anxiety for producing our best performance.

Individuals Capacity for Stress

Despite the fact that some anxiety is necessary and normal to perform any task, in coping with anxiety and stress problems clinically we are usually dealing with levels which are too high. Regardless of who we are or what we may do in life all of us have an upper limit to the stress that our bodies can take. The body may be viewed as a machine, its limitations are finite.

The body's limitations for stress might be compared to all of us having a glass inside our bodies. Every individual has a different upper limit for stress. Therefore all of us will have a different shape and size of our internal stress glass. Since any glass can only take a certain amount of fluid it represents an easy way of thinking of our body's limitations to the amount of stress we can endure. We may extend this metaphor further by suggesting that our everyday experience of stress is rather like a tap which is placed over the glass and into which it drips drops of stress. The more stress we experience, the more the tap drips.

Figure 4.2 The tap and glass – a model of stress

As the level of stress in the system of our bodies rises it becomes increasingly likely that the body will produce physical, mental, or behavioural symptoms, or any combination of these, in response to this stress.

It is important at this point to note that, just as our individual stress glasses are different, so our stress taps and what turns on these taps are different for everyone. Therefore experiences which are stressful for some people will not be perceived as such by others – under the same circumstances some people's taps will turn on and others will remain off.

Symptoms as Signals

The idea behind any signal is that the person who receives it can act upon this information. The symptoms of stress we experience are the body's ways of signalling to us that our stress levels are beginning to get too high. The point at which we receive

Figure 4.3 The level of stress and degree of symptoms

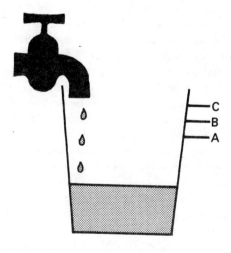

these signals will of course depend upon the size and shape of our internal glasses, that is, it will depend upon our own physiological make-up – our individual capacity for stress.

Gradually, as the stress level in our glass continues to rise, we eventually reach a critical point, some distance from the top of the glass, at which the body begins the signalling process that the stress level is too high. As we have said this signal comes in the form of a physical, mental, or behavioural symptom. Let us say that this critical level is at point A in Figure 4.3. The specific symptom by which our body chooses to signal stress will differ from one individual to the next. For some, the first signal may be a headache, becoming irritable, or feeling low. For others losing sleep, developing obsessional thoughts, or feeling nauseous, and so on. It is very important that all of us learn what our individual specific response to stress may be so that we might learn to respond to this signal early on. In some ways we should consider ourselves lucky if we get these types of responses to stress, because for others, unfortunately, there are other responses to stress that may also occur, such as ulcers and heart disease, from which we may get less warning.

If the signal at point A is ignored, that is, the person does nothing to reduce the stress level then, as the tap keeps dripping, gradually the stress level will continue to rise to say point B. At this stage the original symptom may become worse or another symptom may begin to occur. Again if the signal at B is ignored and stress continues, then gradually the level may continue to rise to point C and once more the original symptom may get worse or change. In this way the person suffering from long-term stress may initially experience, for instance, irritability, then chest pains and then sleep disturbance, or any combination of symptoms. Or they may simply find that their headaches become more frequent and more painful. We must remember that the signals are a means of informing the individual that their stress level is becoming uncomfortably high. The individual must try to act to reduce their level of stress as soon as possible.

Of course our tap may cause the glass to fill up in lots of different ways. It may fill up very slowly and gradually, particularly where stress is constant, such as when work is over demanding, financial problems can't be overcome, or the children are going through a difficult phase. People may then describe symptoms starting 'out of the blue'. Indeed it may seem exactly like this, since after all it is only one more drop of stress, on top of all the other stress accumulated over months and years, which eventually brings the level in the stress glass to a critical point.

Other events may cause the stress tap to turn on much quicker. Our stress levels suddenly rise markedly when we go through a major life event such as perhaps a divorce, serious accident, or death in the family. Alternatively, encountering the situations we fear most will turn on our stress taps rapidly. At such times it may be easier to attribute our stress reaction to these events and so understand more about what is happening.

It is important to realize then that our symptoms, produced in response to stress, are not solely based upon the stress occurring at the given time, but upon all the stress accumulated in our stress glass over time. If, at the start of a difficult problem, the glass is fairly full obviously the body is more likely to signal stress than if the glass is empty. This is why sometimes we can achieve tasks with no difficulty and other times the same task produces anxiety and stress symptoms. Stress can also drain out of the glass as well as drip into it, and the process of overcoming the problems of stress and anxiety is about learning how to turn off the stress tap and drain down the stress glass.

It is important also to note that we are not implying that any major catastrophe will occur should the stress level continue to rise so high that the glass spills over. If this should occur it will only mean that the symptoms will intensify a little further, making it even more difficult to ignore the stress, forcing you to act to reduce the level.

Panic Attacks

Perhaps the most frightening of all the symptoms of stress and anxiety that a person may experience is the panic attack. Its onset is rapid and dramatic, we may get little or no warning, occurring often 'out of the blue' and in situations of no real danger. Not everyone who experiences problems with stress and anxiety will have panic attacks. For those who do their frequency can vary from yearly, to monthly, to many times a day.

For someone who has never had a panic attack it may be

difficult to fully empathize with the client, but it may help if you were to consider the following scenario. Imagine that you are shopping at your local supermarket. You are happily filling your basket with the week's groceries when you turn the corner into the next aisle and suddenly you see a roaring lion, its teeth glistening, open-mouthed and heading straight for you. Of course you'd be panic stricken, your heart would be beating wildly, you would be sweating, shaking, feeling faint, and without a further thought you'd be off like a shot.

Now try to imagine turning into that aisle, all those bodily reactions start to go off, and yet there is nothing there – no lion, nothing for you to be terrified about and yet your heart is beating faster, you're sweating, feeling faint, breathing rapidly, and so on. What would you think? 'I'm going mad, I'm having a heart attack, I'm dying' or at least 'I'm going to make a fool of myself, I'm going to faint or be sick'. Most of us would probably panic, think catastrophic thoughts, breathe rapidly, run away to a safe place, call out the doctor, and make a will. This is often exactly what the panic attack victim thinks and does when they have no idea what is really happening to them.

Unfortunately it is exactly these thoughts and behaviours which make the panic attack worse, make us terrified of having another and make us begin to avoid any and every situation where it could possibly happen again. The more we anticipate the fear reaction the more likely it is that it will occur. Subsequently we look for and find, or even create, the early signals, we magnify these signals, making catastrophic interpretations and predictions which we may or may not be aware of and we may begin to hyperventilate, thereby creating a full-blown panic attack as the stress glass fills rapidly up.

Understanding Panic Attacks – The Alarm Reaction

All of us, given sufficient fright or shock, can experience an alarm reaction. Imagine the physical feeling we would experience if we were high up a ladder and began to feel it slipping, or if we had a 'near miss' in a car. This is the body's sudden and natural response to prepare us to cope with sudden threat. This reponse is entirely automatic, without the need for conscious thought. In order to fully understand an alarm reaction it is useful to think back many thousands of years to the time of the caveman. The experience of a panic attack has its basis in the alarm reaction which may also be known as 'the fight or flight response' discussed in chapter one (Cannon 1929).

Consider the following scenario: a caveman leaves his cave one day setting out in order to hunt for food. As he gets nearer and nearer the jungle in which he will begin hunting, he comes near to a large bush. Suddenly from behind that bush he hears a rustle and some movement, obviously that of an animal. Immediately the caveman must prepare himself for two possibilities. First it may be a rabbit behind the bush making the noise. If that was the case then the caveman's body would need to be ready to dive into the bush, or run after the rabbit, catch it, and kill it for food. The second possibility is that the rustling is a tiger. If this was the case the caveman's body would need to be ready to run away very quickly, or enable him to try to defend himself if caught by the tiger.

In both circumstances we can see that the caveman's body must be prepared, following the initial fright or increase in anxiety, for fight and/or flight. This bodily preparation needs to occur so quickly that there is no time for conscious thought, the caveman does not have time to talk himself into this state of readiness. Rather what happens is that a reflex reaction takes place whereby a signal is sent to the adrenal gland to release the chemical adrenalin into the blood stream. This chemical causes rapid changes to take place within the caveman's body including the following:

Heart rate speeds up   The heart is a pump which pumps blood around the body. In order for muscles to work effectively, to run and fight, they need blood rich in oxygen supplied by the heart.

Breathing rate increases   As the heart speeds up so does the rate of intake of oxygen to supply the blood

Blood is redistributed   Blood is pumped away from areas such as the head and stomach into the long muscles of the body, in the arms and legs. These muscles tense in readiness for action. The caveman does not need to think or use blood in digestive processes, but instead needs it in the arms and legs for running and fighting.

Sweat glands are activated   The caveman's body begins to sweat and it thus becomes wet and slippery. In this way it is more difficult for a tiger to grab hold of. Additionally the sweat serves to cool down the body temperature.

Bowels may be evacuated   The caveman's body may release all waste products, this immediately makes the body feel lighter and assists the caveman to run more quickly.

All the common symptoms of a panic attack can thus be understood in terms of adrenalin being pumped round the body and in terms of the fight/flight mechanism. During a panic attack we may feel our heart beating very fast and very hard, our bodies begin to sweat very heavily, we may feel unreal, faint, dizzy, and nauseous as blood is pumped away from the head and the stomach. We may also feel the need to use the toilet during a severe panic attack and we may find that our breathing pattern changes markedly. All these experiences happen very suddenly and without conscious thought and can be very frightening if we fail to understand what is happening.

A Panic Attack Cannot Harm You.

However frightening a panic attack may be we must always remind ourselves of one fact: none of the symptoms of a panic attack can harm us. People often worry that their heart is beating so fast they will have a heart attack, or they feel so faint and dizzy they will collapse, or they will be physically sick in public. Very often people get so afraid of these consequences that they develop a very serious fear of their own fear response. Therefore, in order to avoid panic attacks, they stop placing themselves in the situations in which they had previously experienced these feelings. As people avoid more and more they become a prisoner of their anxiety.

We must always remember that a panic attack has its basis in the alarm reaction which is a normal bodily mechanism which has helped to keep the species of man alive in situations of danger for thousands of years. If the mechanism made us faint, or vomit, or have a heart attack, then as cavemen we would have made very easy prey every time we encountered an animal we feared. Mankind would have died out long ago if this was the case. It is not and an acute anxiety attack will not harm you.

Hyperventilation and Anxiety Symptoms

Symptoms of a panic attack initiated by adrenalin can never cause us to faint or be sick. However, if we hyperventilate for even brief periods we increase the intensity of the initial symptoms and may bring on these more serious symptoms.

Hyperventilation is a process of breathing rapidly, inhaling and exhaling from the chest rather than from the stomach. This rapid shallow breath may occur in response to the adrenalin which causes the heart to speed up. The faster the heart beats the more rapidly we may be inclined to breathe and the more oxygen we take in. In turn then the heart must beat faster so as to pump blood quicker to cope with all this oxygen coming into the body. Changes in the normal oxygen/carbon dioxide levels occur in the lungs and, in the much longer term, this may have an effect on the acidity of the blood. This may cause a further increase in symptoms, similar to those symptoms of more chronic stress e.g. chest pains, headaches, etc.

A vicious circle is set up. Eventually, if the rapid breathing continues, the body will cut off the excessive supply of oxygen by causing the individual to faint. When we faint we return to normal breathing and so fainting is a fail-safe mechanism for hyperventilation control. If we are prone to hyperventilating during panic attacks, and otherwise at times of increased anxiety, we must learn techniques which help us to breathe more slowly and deeply, from the stomach rather than the chest, and we may also need to rebreathe our own air, breathing into and out of a paper bag, or cupping our hands close to our mouth to catch and rebreathe the exhaled air. This is dealt with in greater detail in chapter five.

Catastrophic Thinking and Anxiety Symptoms

Catastrophic thinking, both in the misinterpretation of bodily symptoms and the anticipation of disaster, plays a central role in the development and exacerbation of anxiety symptoms. There are four types of panic thoughts:

Thoughts of anticipation These type of thoughts put us in the mood to feel anxiety. For example, people with social difficulties may anticipate that there will be nobody at the party who will talk to them. The person who fears dogs may convince him/herself that dogs always bite people, especially them. These thoughts anticipate catastrophe or very unpleasant outcome.

Can't cope thoughts These thoughts relate to both the symptoms and the situations. 'I can't bear this, this is awful'. 'I'll never be able to do it'. 'Everyone can see how anxious I am'. These thoughts serve to reduce our self confidence further and encourage us to give up before trying.

Thoughts misinterpreting bodily sensations These thoughts stem from our misunderstanding of our physical sensations. These include 'I'm having a heart attack', 'I'm going to pass out', 'I'm dying'. These thoughts occur because people imagine something very serious must be wrong with their body to cause the symptoms that they are experiencing. Such catastrophic thoughts are central in increasing our anxiety and thus making the physical symptoms worse.

Escape thoughts These thoughts lead quickly to avoidance of the feared situation and include, 'I'll be OK if I run home now', 'Get away and you'll be all right'. When people listen to these thoughts and avoid or escape, this serves to reduce anxiety. Thus the thought becomes very powerfully strengthened and increases the likelihood of subsequent avoidance.

A Summary – The Acute Anxiety Spiral

We have talked about the experience of anxiety symptoms as being initiated by the sudden or gradual build-up of stress. The tap turns on, either suddenly or slowly, and the glass fills.

As the stress level rises and eventually reaches the individual's critical point a vast array of different physical, mental, or behavioural symptoms will occur to signal stress. One of these possible signals is a panic attack when adrenalin is released into the blood stream and an acute anxiety spiral may then be set into effect. The first stage is a recognition of the initial bodily changes as a result of the adrenalin. These sensations are the first acute symptoms of anxiety, often leading to hyperventilation and to the initiation of catastrophic panic thoughts. The second stage is an awareness of, not only the situation we find difficult or are afraid of, but also of the fact that we are becoming anxious and beginning to panic. This leads to a bigger surge of anxiety, we become anxious about becoming anxious. The third stage is seeing our anxiety getting bigger and bigger and this makes it get worse. This is illustrated diagrammatically in Figure 4.4.

Figure 4.4 The acute anxiety spiral

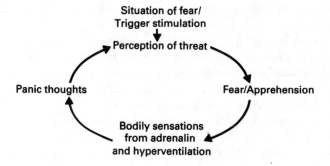

How Does Anxiety Start?

The simple answer to this question is that there may be lots of ways in which anxiety may develop. We have suggested that the experience of physical symptoms of anxiety result from stress. This may be from chronic stress, where our stress tap drips constantly a small amount at a time for months or years, or from sudden stress, when we encounter a specific fear, problem or major life event, which causes the stress tap to turn full on. The specific nature of the stress will vary enormously from one individual to another as will their specific symptomatic response.

Certain types of fears are very common when we are children. Around 90 per cent of children between the ages of 5 and 12 years admit to having specific fears such as fear of animals, strange situations, fear of noise, and the dark. These tend to disappear as we grow older but occasionally persist into adulthood. Other fears may be caused by unpleasant shock or injury. Examples might be the lift phobic who was once trapped in a lift, or the water phobic who once very nearly drowned. Some fears can begin by seeing unpleasant things happen to others, or may be copied from other people, such as our parents. Also any major life event is stressful and this experience may precipitate the first symptoms of anxiety. Some people may exhibit a general anxiety. These may be people who seem to have always been anxious, people with a predisposition to worry. Others may have been maintaining a stressful lifestyle for years, always rushing onwards, filling their time with one impossible task after the next.

For some clients, understanding the origins of their fears and stress is easy, for others many sessions of assessment and detailed analysis may not result in any certainty as to the genesis of their problems. Many clients can become frustrated by this fact, believing that there must be some very significant detail in their past which has caused them to become anxious or stressed currently. The model of the tap and the glass however explains that for some people their first experience of anxiety symptoms was not caused by any specific frightful encounter but rather by the insidious, unapparent build-up of stress, one drop at a time. The final drop was no more significant in stress terms than any of the thousands of previous drops. It just happened to be the one which caused the glass to become overfilled and which caused the body to begin to signal being under excessive stress.

Therefore, when clients relate their first and subsequent panic attacks, or other symptoms of anxiety and stress, and explain that they were doing nothing out of the ordinary, it is entirely possible that this was the case.

One very important fact to establish at the outset, therefore, is that it is not necessary to know why a particular fear or problem started in order to overcome it.

What Maintains Anxiety?

Though it may be very difficult to establish what has triggered our first experience of anxiety, we know a lot more about what factors cause the stress tap to remain turned on, preventing the anxiety from ever going away spontaneously. Basically there are a number of general factors which can serve to maintain anxiety.

How Lifestyle Maintains Anxiety

This includes the particular stressful lifestyle we may have become locked into. It is useful to think of how we cope with the stresses of life as a set of scales (see Figure 4.5). On one side of the scales are our resources and on the other side the demands that life places upon us.

Figure 4.5 Resources versus demands

1. Physical health
2. Skills and experience
3. Emotional make-up/ Personality
4. Social support
5. Opportunities for pleasure/relaxation
6. Positive and realistic attitudes and expectations

1. Demands of life: emotional, physical, financial, social
2. Adjustment to change: work, illness, unemployment, marriage
3. Unrealistic and negative attitudes and expectations of self and others

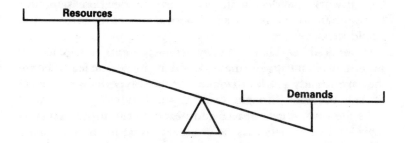

Obviously if the demands upon us outweigh our resources this will create stress and will continue to do so until we act either to strengthen our resources or reduce the demands upon us or both. Stress will be maintained for as long as the balance measures demands to be greater than resources.

Another way of thinking of this is to return to the tap metaphor and to see that the tap represents demands and the glass represents resources. As the glass fills and demands increase so eventually demands will get very close to, and eventually outstretch our resources, producing stress and physical symptoms which occur to signal this fact.

How Avoidance Maintains Anxiety

Another behavioural pattern which maintains anxiety is avoidance. Initially as a result of the fear reaction it seems that people avoid the situations which induced their fear or high levels of stress. However, the more we investigate this phenomenon with the client the more often it becomes clear that the avoidance is maintained because the person is afraid of the fear response itself. Basically they become terrified of having another anxiety attack. This is fear of fear.

Perhaps this can be made clearer by taking the specific example of somebody who has an anxiety attack whilst shopping in a supermarket. It is important to note that we could have chosen any example of a stressful situation with which a person is having problems. This may include avoiding facing up to the boss at work, avoiding going to a party or social occasion, and many other situations. For all of these examples the information would look the same.

If we look at Figure 4.6, which represents a trip to the supermarket, it suggests that by the time the person leaves home they are already a little anxious about the trip perhaps as a result of their previous difficulties with this task.

As the person gets nearer and nearer to the supermarket so their level of anxiety may be gradually rising in anticipation of difficulty. The more the level of their anxiety rises the more the person will panic, further increasing the anxiety. Eventually, still some distance from the supermarket perhaps, the person's level of anxiety may become so high that they imagine that any further increase will have a catastrophic effect on them. For

Figure 4.6 Avoidance and anxiety levels

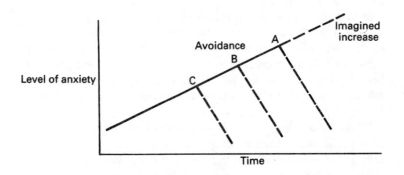

example, they feel that they will faint, be sick, have a heart attack, or imagine they are going to die. The person feels totally unable to take any more of these feelings and imagines that the feelings themselves will get much worse. Thus at this imaginary point A they give up, turn around, and go home. This causes an immediate reduction in anxiety so in a sense the person is rewarded for running away.

The next time they are able to gather together enough courage to set out for the supermarket they may get only as far as point B before they have had enough, anticipating more extreme levels of anxiety if they continue. On the next occasion they may get only as far as point C and so on until they are virtually unable to leave home. Being terrified of a reoccurence of the frightening physical symptoms, thus the avoidance becomes one of the fear response itself. Anticipating extremely high levels of anxiety, the person no longer encounters the original situation of the supermarket. Additionally the fear may 'generalize' so that a person becomes afraid of all shops, not just supermarkets, and then cinemas, and then restaurants, and so on.

How Loss of Confidence Maintains Anxiety

A person's confidence stems very largely from seeing him/herself cope effectively with all of life's everyday demands and challenges. The confident person is happy to try new things because in the past they have had success at similar related tasks. The degree to which a person feels confident at performing any given task can in some ways be thought of as a 'circle of safety' (see Figure 4.7). A person full of confidence feels safe in having a go at most things, their circle of safety is thus very large, they can perform the given task anytime anywhere. For people with anxiety problems however it is common for their confidence to become slowly eroded. They begin to avoid difficult situations and tasks because they lack the self-confidence to deal with them effectively.

This can be illustrated using an imaginary person with a fear of supermarkets. Initially they could get as far as point A, then only as far as point B, and then only as far as point C. Thus the circle of safety tends to diminish gradually. Eventually, if this person continues to avoid without receiving any help they may become housebound altogether.

Figure 4.7 Confidence and circles of safety

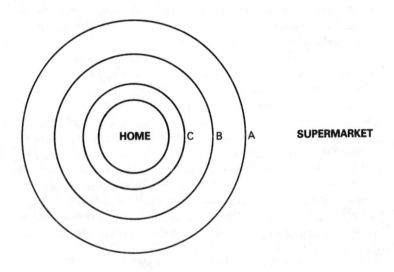

We could take many such examples of avoidance. At work a person may avoid big meetings, then smaller meetings, then talking with the boss, and eventually talking to anyone. Socially a person may first avoid theatres and cinemas, then parties and dinners, then pubs, and then going out altogether. In every case the person's repertoire is gradually restricted, their confidence is eaten away, and they will lose all hope of ever being able to do these things again, and eventually stop trying altogether. It is extremely important that the client must learn that avoidance of difficult situations is never an appropriate solution for their anxiety.

How Our Thinking Maintains Anxiety

Thinking and acute anxiety We have already discussed this in relation to the acute anxiety spiral but it is well worth repeating that avoidance, prior to encountering the full experience of the feared situation, occurs because of what the person believes is going to happen. Examples of this may be: the agoraphobic person who never goes out because they believe they will collapse and die of a heart attack; the lift phobic who believes they may become trapped in the lift and suffocate to death; a person who avoids meeting others because, if a disagreement starts, they believe they will lose their temper and hit people; and last, a person may obsessively check the locks on doors and windows, believing that somebody is bound to break into the house if they fail to make these checks.

These examples help us to establish three things:

1 People with anxiety disorders may have exaggerated, irrational beliefs concerning the consequences of facing up to the feared or difficult situation.
2 They are prone to making catastrophic misinterpretations of their symptoms, thereby making them more frightening and increasing panic. Anxious people become acutely sensitized to their bodies, noticing minor bodily changes upon which they focus. They are constantly looking for these changes, especially in situations which have previously been difficult.
3 Because people avoid these situations, they are unable to overcome their irrational beliefs since they are never proved wrong.

81

In the development of fears and other difficulties one thing is certain, thinking in these ways leads to avoidance of the problem situation. If we avoid facing up to it we then make it more likely that the next time the situation, or a similar one, is encountered we will avoid it again.

Very commonly anxious and stressed people express thoughts of self-doubt and self-deprecation. As anxiety takes over their lives they feel imprisoned and unable to break free. They may say they've 'failed', they're 'hopeless and helpless'. The more people say such things to themselves the more these thoughts become automatic and fixed, and the less they are able to see a future for themselves. They may adopt a generally negative outlook on life, tending to anticipate and see problems where none exist, finding things to worry about. They may also become dependent upon medication, or other people, as they lose the confidence to cope for themselves.

Perfectionist and obsessional thoughts can also increase stress and cause loss of confidence. Setting unrealistic standards means we can only fail, nothing we do is ever enough or exactly right. We can never be satisfied, gradually eroding our self-esteem and confidence further.

THE TREATMENT PROGRAMME: TURNING OFF THE TAP AND DRAINING THE GLASS

Understanding What is Happening

Before we undertake any active treatment it is essential that we have helped the client to understand that excessive stress leads to symptoms of anxiety. Anxiety is not a single entity but rather comprises three facets: first, the way we *feel*, meaning our physical sensations, including both acute and chronic symptoms; second, the way we *think*, including catastrophic, irrational and negative thoughts; third, the way we *behave*, including patterns of avoidance and stressful lifestyles. Helping the client to reassess their difficulties in these terms helps to specify and clarify the exact nature of these problems and highlight the specific areas of change required.

The client must be helped to be able to rationalize and accept their symptoms as natural bodily processes – a signal to reduce stress, rather than a signal of impending doom.

Intellectual acceptance of what is going on is, however, rarely enough. Many clients tell us that deep down they know a panic attack, or any particular acute symptom of anxiety, is not harmful but they are still unable to overcome their fears.

Having educated our clients in relation to the psychology and physiology of anxiety, the next step is to help them break any patterns of avoidance that may have become established. Therapy teaches clients that feelings can be tolerated and will fade away if they stay in the feared or difficult situation. Anxiety symptoms do not go on increasing indefinitely.

Let us reconsider the example of the person who is afraid of shopping in the supermarket (see Figure 4.8).

Figure 4.8 Levels of anxiety staying in the feared situation

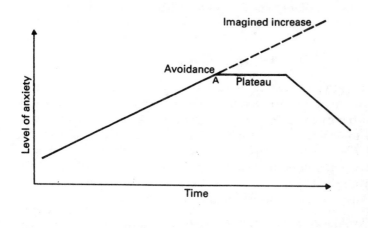

The person avoided the situation at point A, believing that their anxiety was going to keep on going up along the dotted line. We know however that what actually happens is that the anxiety only ever reaches a certain level and then levels off, forming a plateau. This occurs because there is a limit to the amount of physiological change in the body that adrenalin can produce.

When the anxiety upper limit is reached it will remain at this level for a certain time. This time will depend largely upon what the person feels and thinks and how they behave. If they allow themselves to continually think catastrophic thoughts, or focus too much on the symptoms themselves, or race up and down, or hyperventilate, the plateau time will last much longer. If they are able to think positive coping thoughts, control breathing, distract themselves from their symptoms, and try to relax, other symptoms will quickly die away.

After some time, if a person stays within the difficult situation, the brain and body will begin to realize there is no real danger and the supply of adrenalin to the blood stream will be cut off. Then gradually the person's level of anxiety will fall back to normal levels from point B in Figure 4.8.

Obviously a person who has spent all their life avoiding such situations will never have had the opportunity to learn about the plateau stage and the gradual fading away of anxiety. Therefore, a very important part of the treatment programme must be helping the client to face up to their fear and stay in the difficult situation learning that they can control their anxiety.

Specifying the Problem Areas

During the assessment phase it is very important that the client must attempt to specify any particular situations or difficulties which create problems currently and which in the past may have led to avoidance. This list is probably much easier to compile for clients who experience phobic problems, but people with more generalized anxiety and stress will often report avoiding certain situations.

A typical list of difficulties might be as follows:

1 Avoidance of all public transport, i.e. buses and trains.
2 Fear of flying.
3 Marital problems.
4 Difficulty talking to the boss.
5 Sexual problems.
6 Difficulty with social situations, e.g. going to parties.

The client may then be asked to re-order this list in terms of the most and least pressing problems. In this way they may indicate a preference as to which particular difficulty will be

Figure 4.9 Anxiety related to buses

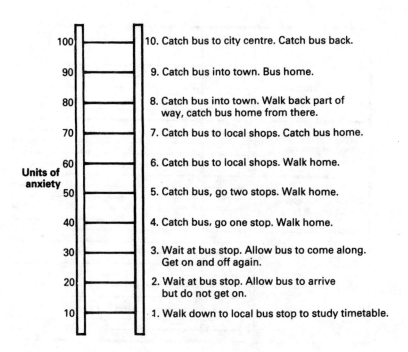

addressed first. Allowing the client to choose in this way can often increase their motivation for the success of the treatment. However, the therapist must be careful not to give the client an entirely free choice if it is believed that one, or a combination, of the client's difficulties are central in maintaining the others. If, for instance, the therapist believes that the client's marital problems are undermining their confidence and feelings of security, and it is this that prevents the client from achieving other tasks, then the therapist's endeavours should be aimed at this problem first.

Constructing a Programme for Overcoming Anxiety – Gradual Exposure

Let us suppose the client suggests that they first wish to overcome their difficulties in using public transport, specifically

Figure 4.10 Bus programme for Mr Smith

Target	Date/ time	How Did it Go?	Rate Anxiety 1–100
1. Walk to local Bus Stop to study time-table	1 2 3 4 5		
2. Wait at bus stop. Allow bus to arrive, don't get on.	1 2 3 4 5		
3. Wait at bus stop. Get on and off again.	1 2 3 4 5		
4. Catch bus, go 1 stop. Walk home.	1 2 3 4 5		
5. Catch bus, go 2 stops. Walk home.	1 2 3 4 5		

buses. The therapist believes this problem is maintained independently of the client's other problems and thus accepts this as the first goal for therapy. The principles for overcoming any of the six problem areas listed previously can be adapted to the following general format. First, the problem is broken down into smaller targets or stages. Usually around ten steps are constructed each one slightly more demanding than the former. The final step or target is the eventual goal or level of performance to which the client aspires. The earlier steps are gradually closer approximations to this goal (see Figure 4.9).

The stages in this programme may be compared to the steps of a ladder. A scale of anxiety or perceived difficulty is then established from zero (no anxiety) to 100 (maximum anxiety).

Each task is then rated on this scale. Through careful negotiation with the client it is important that each stage on the programme is designed to be only approximately ten units of anxiety or difficulty greater than the previous stage. Thus the stages of the progamme may be spaced almost exactly equally, like the steps on a ladder.

The top of the ladder is the eventual target of the programme but we can never climb a ladder starting at the top. Likewise we will not be successful if the client is sent away expected to achieve the most difficult target first. With guidance the client will learn to climb the ladder gradually starting at the bottom one rung at a time.

The next stage is to make each step of the ladder a specific target. It is useful for the client to keep a record of success and failure and this can be done as in Figure 4.10.

Each target is attempted five times in Figure 4.10 within a specific time period, usually a week. It is hoped that initially the client will experience some anxiety with each target and learn to cope with this effectively, but that over five attempts of this target this anxiety will drop to a minimum. This will only occur if the client stays with the experience of anxiety and does not

Figure 4.11 Target 1: Going to the bus stop to study time-table

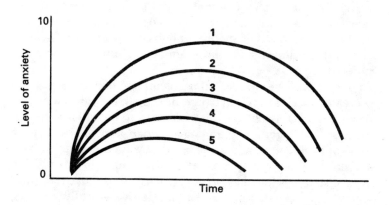

87

avoid the situation. The client's experience of anxiety for each of the five trials of each target may be represented graphically as in Figure 4.11.

The client is required to rate their anxiety on the programme chart after each trial on a scale of 1–100, where 1 is no anxiety and 100 is maximum anxiety. The therapist must ensure that the client's ratings of anxiety are as accurate as possible by discussing them in detail with the client. The client should not proceed onto the next target until anxiety levels are low, usually below 20 or 30 units on the previous target.

If necessary more than five trials can be used if the level of anxiety fails to come down on any one specific target. Finally, if levels are still high it is probably because the target is too difficult and an intermediate, less difficult, target must be inserted and overcome first. Re-negotiation of steps is very commonly required since theoretical assumptions of difficulty are often not mirrored by experience in practice. As each target is completed the client encounters the next, until all targets are overcome. Several programme sheets will be required.

As the anxiety for each target is overcome so the client is only ever raising their anxiety by ten units by going onto the next target. Effectively, every time the client takes another step on the ladder this becomes the bottom step, only approximately ten units of anxiety off the ground. Thus the ladder is sinking into the ground one step at a time as the client climbs on to it. Gradually, the client's confidence grows as they regularly list their successes. Early achievement spurs the client on; they are taught to focus on their success, and to cope with any difficulties rationally by altering the programme slightly until success is achieved.

For others of the six original problems mentioned it is possible to create stages to effect change in exactly the same way. For instance marital problems can often lead to not talking, spending less time together, planning separate lives. These can be forms of avoidance that make it impossible for the couple to look at their marital problems. Getting the couple to write down targets, stating what they want to change in the marriage and negotiating these targets, can be an effective way of improving the situation. Likewise, the therapeutic techniques for overcoming sexual problems often involve a graded series of targets towards improving performance and technique one stage at a time. The number of steps to the ladder and number of trials for each step is negotiable, but the general principle of graded systematic exposure, facing up to the difficulty and learning to cope with it, holds for each of these cases.

Self-Help Skills

In addition to the process of education and a negotiated programme for overcoming the chosen difficulty, the client is taught a number of specific skills which will assist them to combat and overcome their feelings of anxiety. These skills include: teaching the client to relax; teaching techniques of distraction to help the client focus their attention away from physical sensations and negative thoughts; teaching skills of positive and rational thinking – also an important aspect of control; and teaching breathing control skills to offset the likelihood of the client exacerbating their physical symptoms through hyperventilation.

Anxiety is like a smouldering fire, a wind can come along and ignite the glowing embers. When this happens, some people respond by pouring paraffin over that fire, turning it into a blazing inferno (i.e. panicking, hyperventilating, catastrophizing, avoiding, etc.), while others sensibly dampen down the blaze with a wet blanket (i.e. relaxing, thinking positively, goal planning, problem solving, and self assertion). These self-help skills are dealt with in the next two chapters.

Changing Lifestyles

Nobody will be able to fully overcome their anxiety without changing lifestyles. The way that the client has been behaving, thinking and feeling up until the point of therapy was clearly too stressful, therefore change is necessary. If the client is overworking, has taken on too many commitments, has no fun or pleasure in life, or sets him/herself totally unrealistic goals, then these behaviours and attitudes must be changed. No anxiety management techniques will work against these odds, just as aspirins will not control headaches if a person continues to bang their head against the wall. Chapter 6 deals with changes in lifestyle in greater detail.

Common Questions About Anxiety

Advantages and Disadvantages of Medication

Sometimes clients will be offered tranquillizers in order to help them overcome their difficulties. In relation to the tap and glass metaphor we can think of these as being something like a plunger that fits over the glass and which forces down the level of stress. Unfortunately, as the tranquillizer wears off so the plunger gradually slides back up and the former level of stress returns. Also, the more tranquillizers are used, the older and less effective the plunger becomes, therefore, gradually, the same dose of tablets becomes less and less effective.

Another way of looking at tranquillizer use is to think of the following analogy: you are driving along the motorway and suddenly your car oil warning light comes on. Instead of pulling over onto the hard shoulder, opening the car bonnet and putting more oil in the engine, you take a hammer and bash out the oil warning light. We must learn to see our anxiety symptoms as signals that we are under stress and learn to cope with and control these signals through our efforts and not simply mask or try to ignore them with tranquillizers.

Despite these facts there may be a case for a short-term course of tablets, or the occasional use of a tablet to help us through a particularly difficult situation and to help build confidence. This will only happen, however, if such situations are approached subsequently with decreasing amounts of assistance from medication.

Why do I Feel Better One Day and Worse the Next?

Fluctuations in mood are perfectly normal. However, if we are attempting to overcome fear using a specific programme of targets, these fluctuations make similar targets more difficult on some days than others. Unfortunately, anxious and stressed people become acutely sensitive to such fluctuations making them worse by their own concern. It is important not to let these experiences get you down. It is more important to achieve a difficult target on a bad day than a good one because it will increase your confidence still further. It is very important not to simply write it off completely as 'a bad day' just because things have gone wrong. We must keep trying and looking for successes, however small.

It is also very important for you to reward yourself when you have had some success. All of us are very good at blaming ourselves if things go wrong and feeling upset, but we must be fair with ourselves and take the credit when things go well. So remember to treat yourselves, perhaps slowly saving up and buying a present for yourself or doing things you enjoy, as rewards for your achievements.

How Long Will it Take?

Nobody could possibly offer a definite answer to this and say how long it may take to fully overcome anxiety and stress problems. We do know however that, with perseverance, every day can produce some success and that, by continuing to work one day at a time, we will be building up a very solid basis for renewed confidence and further achievement. It will certainly not seem long if you work consistently toward daily targets, in a few weeks you'll be doing things you haven't done for years, or never thought possible. However small these daily achievements may seem they are one more step up the ladder to freedom from your fears and problems.

Chapter Five

SELF–HELP TECHNIQUES EXPLAINED

INTRODUCTION

There is no single self-help procedure which will act as a panacea in the management of anxiety and stress. Rather, in addition to the important process of education and understanding, the combination of behavioural and cognitive techniques, together with the client's changes in lifestyle, will offer a cumulative process of management and gradual amelioration of anxiety. It is important that some referring agents are dissuaded from a popular belief that anxiety management equals relaxation training or any single technique. This belief may serve to minimize and underestimate the experience of anxiety in the eyes of the referring agent and the client, the latter becoming quickly dispirited, losing faith in themselves, the specific technique, or the skill of the therapist.

This chapter aims to offer the reader an introduction to the most common self-help techniques taught to clients in anxiety management training. Though some theory is presented for each, the bulk of the information is the basic practical information and skills imparted to the client. Much of this information is offered in the form that the authors give to their clients in written handouts.

RELAXATION TRAINING

The use of relaxation as a means of anxiety and stress management is not a new phenomenon. Many Eastern religions have been using techniques such as yoga and meditation for many centuries and both of these techniques hold much common ground with modern clinical relaxation methods.

Theoretical Basis of Relaxation Training

Relaxation induces physiological effects opposite in nature to those induced by psychological stress. Specifically relaxation produces a decrement in sympathetic nervous system activity and causes an increase in parasympathetic nervous system activity. Relaxation therefore serves to lower the heart rate, reduce blood pressure, reduce sweat gland activity, alter brain wave pattern, and reduce somatomotor activity.

Additionally, those relaxation techniques which incorporate muscle tensing exercises, aim to teach the client to become generally more aware of the experience of muscular tension. The client is taught to self-monitor and become aware of, for example, gripping the car steering wheel too tightly, grinding their jaws, or feeling tense in the back of the neck. In this way the client begins to realize that their former 'resting state' may have been fraught with muscular tensions serving to exacerbate the general experience of anxiety and stress.

Relaxation training is a skill, a learned response, which the client can use to combat the experience of stress and feelings of anxiety. With practice people can become proficient at recognizing and turning off the tension within the body for themselves without drugs.

Progressive Muscular Relaxation (PMR)

Many of the current clinical methods of relaxation training are based upon the techniques of Jacobson (1938). Modern routine clinical practice however offers something of a dilution of the original Jacobsonian relaxation techniques. Constrained by time and numbers of referrals it is usual to teach relaxation techniques over one to three sessions, with occasional revision practice at later dates. Practitioners vary in their technique but most use fewer muscle groups and exercises than the original procedures. The authors' procedures, presented later, rely upon twenty muscle groups and involve hypnotic-type suggestion to enhance the physical experience of relaxation. High

93

expectations are set up for the client to gradually learn to achieve deep feelings of heaviness and relaxation throughout the body.

PMR – Instruction Handout for Clients

Why Should I Learn to Relax?

Relaxation exercises are designed to help you learn how to reduce muscular tension and to become generally more aware of tension in your body. By learning to produce muscular tension through tensing exercises and then releasing this tension, you will gradually find it is possible to release the physical tension from everyday stress in the same way, letting go. Learning to relax is like pulling a plug at the bottom of your stress glass, gradually the tension and stress drain away. Feeling relaxed will help you to think in a more relaxed way and this will help you to behave in a more relaxed manner. Each of these things will assist in turning off the stress tap.

What Will I Feel from Relaxation?

As you tense a system of muscles, blood, containing oxygen, is selectively pumped into this area of the body to assist the use of the muscles. On releasing this tension two things will happen. First as the flow of blood is reduced the change in blood supply may produce a slight tingling sensation in this muscle group. Second, as the tension is released and the muscles go limp they become effectively dead weight hanging upon the bones of the skeleton. The exercises of relaxation then are gradually causing more and more muscles to act as dead weight, sagging down, hanging on the skeleton causing the weight and heaviness of the body to be seeming to increase gradually as we become increasingly relaxed.

High levels of tension can lead to rigid control; some people when learning to relax report being afraid to go too deeply into the exercises for fear of losing control. It is important to understand that you will always remain in ultimate control when relaxing and that you can always stop the proceedings at any time should they become unpleasant or uncomfortable. Realizing this will gradually help you to gain confidence to go deeper and deeper into relaxation and experience full benefit from it.

Conditions Required for Relaxation

Relaxation, like any skill, takes time and practice to learn. Significant and lasting gains can be achieved by most people within a month with thirty minutes of daily practice. The best time to practice relaxation is when you are feeling most under stress but often this is not convenient. Don't stick to a single time each day but try to vary it to see if the time of day makes a difference for you. Don't be put off if relaxation doesn't seem to work immediately for you. Give it time, practice is essential.

You can perform relaxation exercises lying down but we would prefer if you try initially sitting in a comfortable arm-chair. The seated position corresponds more readily to our body posture during the day when stress develops. Make sure you won't be disturbed. Sit in a warm quiet room and turn off all bright lights. Close your eyes to perform the exercises. This will reduce distractions and help you concentrate upon your bodily feelings.

Before the exercises actually begin, for a few minutes, close your eyes and breathe through your nose. Breathe slowly and deeply trying to breathe from your stomach, lifting your chest to let more air in. Do not strain. With practice this form of breathing will come naturally to you. Say the word 'calm' in your mind each time you breathe out. By doing this your muscles will gradually begin to relax and feelings of calm and heaviness will develop naturally. When you have finished all the exercises return to the word 'calm', saying it in your mind each time you breathe out. Gradually in this way an association will develop between the word 'calm' and the feelings of deep muscle relaxation in your body, so that eventually just closing your eyes and thinking the word 'calm' can induce these feelings.

The PMR Tensing Exercises

The exercises as taught by the authors focus on twenty different groups of muscles. They begin in the person's dominant hand. The exercises proceed up one arm and are then repeated for the other arm. From here exercises focus in the top of the head and follow a logical course down the body finally to the toes. The exercises are described for a right handed person as follows:

95

Area	Muscular Exercise
1 Right Hand	Clench right fist
2 Right forearm	Bend back right hand at right angles to arm
3 Right bicep	Force knuckles of right hand onto right shoulder
4 Left hand	Clench left fist
5 Left forearm	Bend back left hand at right angles to arm
6 Left bicep	Force knuckles of left hand onto left shoulder
7 Forehead	Raise eyebrow up Frown, forcing eyebrows down
8 Eyes	Screw eyes up tightly
9 Mouth, cheeks, jaw	Clench teeth and stretch mouth in exaggerated smile
10 Back of neck	Gently force head back
11 Front of neck, chin	Force chin down onto chest
12 Shoulders/back	Force shoulders forward Force shoulders backwards
13 Chest/back	Take in deep breath, hold it, force chest to expand
14 Stomach	Suck in stomach muscles under rib cage
15 Right thigh	Straighten right leg, lift off ground
16 Right calf	Bend down right foot, bend down toes
17 Right ankle/foot	Bend up right foot, curl up toes
18 Left thigh	Straighten left leg, lift off ground
19 Left calf	Bend down left foot, bend down toes
20 Left ankle/foot	Bend up left foot, bend up toes

Each exercise is designed to create tension within a specific muscle group.

If you fail to experience tension you must try to develop your own exercise which serves to tense that particular muscle group.

Tensing the muscle groups Hold each tensing exercise for approximately five seconds then release the tension immediately *not* gradually. Just stop tensing and let the muscles relax with gravity. Repeat each exercise twice with a ten second gap in-between. Focus on the feelings of tension and relaxation, learn the difference between these two sensations.

Try not to tense the muscles so hard that you produce cramp or pain. Ease up if this happens. Try to tense only the one specific area at a time, e.g. do not clench your teeth and contort your face if you're trying to create tension in the hand by squeezing your fist.

Finally, if you find your mind wanders on to other thoughts during the exercise bring it back to focus on the feelings. If you feel tired do not attempt the exercises. You will learn nothing if you fall asleep. As each tensing exercise is released feel the heaviness develop in that muscle group. A calm relaxing feeling flows throughout the body as though lead weights were slowly pulling the body down into the chair, heavier and heavier, more and more calm at every moment.

An Example Part Script for PMR Training In Vivo

'Settle back as comfortably as you can ... and as you relax in the chair concentrate upon your breathing, breathing in and out through your nose and from your stomach ... lift your chest to allow your lungs to fill ... in and out ... slowly and smoothly. And now each time you breathe out think the word "calm" in your mind ... each time you think the word calm so the body will relax a little more, become slightly more heavy and sink down deeper and deeper into the chair ... and just go on now in silence for a minute or so thinking the word "calm" and relaxing the body in preparation for the exercises of relaxation ...'

[One to two-minute break]

'Now I would like you to stop focussing upon the word "calm" and instead turn your attention to your right hand ... we are now going to create a sensation of tension in your right hand by making a fist. Do this now. Squeeze your fist ... study the feelings of tension this creates ... learn what it is like now to have this experience of tension in the fist ... [after approximately five seconds] ... and now relax ... let go of all the tension just allow your fingers to fall with gravity ... you may experience a slight tingling effect as the muscles relax ... feel the fingers and hand becoming heavier and heavier ... feeling as though someone has just placed a glove made of lead on your hand ... causing the whole hand to feel heavy, heavy as lead ... the muscles sinking down dead weight hanging on the bones of the hand ... [After ten seconds] And now we are going to create tension again in your right hand by making a fist ... Do this now.'

The procedure of tensing and relaxing follows this general form of monolgue for each of the twenty muscle groups. The suggestions of heaviness, reference to lead weights, and the body sinking down under this weight continue throughout the procedure. The client is also constantly reminded to study and learn the sensation of tension, to develop awareness in the resting state. At the end of the exercise they return to the word 'calm' for approximately five minutes. In total the full exercise will take approximately thirty minutes. Finally, the client is told to stretch all of his muscles, as though waking from a deep sleep, to gradually open their eyes, and get up slowly.

Speeding Up the Process of PMR

As the clients relaxation skills develop the exercises may be combined so as to speed up the process of relaxation.

The twenty original muscle groups may be combined, as follows, into seven separate exercises.

Areas	Muscular Exercise
1 Muscles of right arm	Clenched right fist is forced onto right shoulder
2 Muscles of left arm	Clenched left fist is forced onto left shoulder
3 Muscles of face	Frown, screw up eyes, clench teeth, stretch mouth
4 Muscles of neck/ chin	Shoulders brought up head forced down
5 Shoulders, chest, stomach	Shoulders forced back, chest expanded, stomach sucked in
6 Right leg	Straighten right leg, force foot down, and toes down
7 Left leg	Straighten left leg, force foot down, curl toes down

Finally, having practiced with the above procedure for some months, all exercises may be combined, contracting all muscle groups simultaneously. Hold the tension for about ten seconds, and relax. Repeat three times.

Variations and Additions to PMR

Comparing in Vivo and Tape-recorded PMR Training

Amost all experimental studies have shown in vivo training to be superior to the use of tape recorded instructions. As a bare minimum it is suggested that the therapist must talk the client through these techniques at least once before offering the client a tape. In this way the therapist can observe and explain away any difficulties the client may have and reinforce the benefits of the technique. Also the procedures may be tapered and modified at the outset to meet the needs of the individual.

The sole use of a tape may lead to 'tape dependence' the client being unable to relax without the tape. The client must proceed at the speed of the tape rather than in their own time. If possible the therapist should make their own tape of relaxation instructions which assists in the transfer of the skills from the therapy session to the home situation.

Biofeedback Apparatus

Biofeedback has been shown to act as a useful adjunct to relaxation training and can be particularly useful for focal areas of tension in the body. There are a number of different possible ways of using biofeedback apparatus in assisting clients to relax. Basically the procedure involves monitoring biological signals that come from the central nervous system, the autonomic nervous system, the musculoskeletal system and the cardiovascular system. Different biofeedback apparatus is used depending upon which system is being monitored.

In relaxation we may wish to monitor brain wave activity using an electroencephalograph (EEG) and would expect to find a shift in brain wave pattern toward synchronized high voltage, low frequency waves as the client relaxes. We may also monitor the electrical activity of the muscles using an electromyograph (EMG) and would find reduced activity as the muscles relax. A slowing of the heart with relaxation might be monitored by an electrocardiograph (ECG), and a reduction in sweat gland activity monitored using apparatus measuring skin conductance levels (SCL). Each of these signals can be fed back either visually or, perhaps more usefully to the client, audibly. Their task becomes one of being able to reduce the tone or number of audible clicks as they relax more and more deeply.

Other forms of Relaxation

There are obviously many and various different techniques for relaxation. The authors have chosen to present PMR since it is this method that we use most often. We do not imply that PMR is necessarily the most effective technique for any one individual client but the scope of this book does not extend to covering all possible relaxation techniques.

CONTROLLING HYPERVENTILATION

A sudden sensation of tightness in the throat, gasping for breath, rapid shallow breathing, feeling faint, dizzy, and hot. This might be a typical presentation of acute hyperventilation caused by rapid shallow breathing during moments of high anxiety. However, for others the condition may present in a far more insidious and subtle manner, the constant yawning or sighing, the one deep breath in three, excessive sniffing, each of these may account for the reduced levels of carbon dioxide in the lungs, which over time leads to the 'chronic hyperventilation syndrome'. This may produce a vast array of physical symptoms including numbness or tingling in toes and fingers, tinnitus, headache and severe chest pains. The symptoms of hyperventilation can therefore mimic virtually all the symptoms also attributed to anxiety and chronic stress.

What Happens if I Hyperventilate? (Client Handout)

Hyperventilation is a process of rapid shallow breathing from the upper chest. It occurs fairly commonly during anxiety attacks because some degree of rapid breathing is part of the body's natural response to threat, to increase the intake of oxygen to supply the muscles. If the extra oxygen taken in is not needed by the muscles for running away or fighting, the effects can be dramatic. These may include:

Increase in heart rate
Sweating
Tingling or numbness
Muscle tension and rigidity
Feeling faint
Hot and/or cold flushes
Difficulty getting breath
Tightness of chest
Feelings of being suffocated

Rapid breathing causes the balance of gases in the lungs to alter. Breathing in too much air effectively pushes out carbon dioxide which normally forms a reservoir in the lungs. The physical symptoms occur as a result of too much oxygen and too little carbon dioxide.

How to Control Acute Hyperventilation

There are two aspects to controlling hyperventilation:

1 Stop the rapid over breathing
2 Replenish the carbon dioxide supplies in the lungs

You must learn to become aware of your pattern of breathing when you first start to become anxious. Look out for the early warning signals of over-breathing like feelings of tightness in the chest, or feelings of being stifled – difficulty getting your breath.

As soon as you notice that you are breathing rapidly:

1 Stop whatever you are doing and try to find a quiet place to sit down.
2 Close your eyes and focus on the word 'calm' in your mind.
3 Try to release some of the tension in the upper body. Sitting in a tense hunched-up position increases the possibility of hyperventilation. Dropping shoulders in a sideways widening direction makes hyperventilation more difficult since the chest and diagphragm muscles are stretched outwards.
4 Breathe slowly from the stomach *not* the chest – breathing in to a count of four slowly and out to a count of four slowly, or visualize your breathing-in as going up one side of a hill, experiencing the plateau at the top and then breathing-out as though coming down the other side.
5 It may help to place your hands with your fingertips together

on your stomach – make sure each time you breathe in your fingertips come apart and come together as your breathe out. In this way you will be sure that you are breathing from the stomach.

6 Concentrate on breathing out.

If your symptoms don't go away after a few minutes it is probable that you haven't caught it quickly enough and in this case you will need to use the technique of 'rebreathing'. This involves breathing in the air you have just breathed out. This air is richer in carbon dioxide and it will thus quickly replenish the carbon dioxide you have been blowing off. In order to rebreathe, make a loose mask over your face with your hands (see Figure 5.1).

Figure 5.1 The rebreathing technique

As you breathe out you will trap some of this air in this mask and slowly breathe it back in. Breathe in through the nose and out hard through the mouth, both to a slow count of four. A paper bag (not polythene) may be used instead of a hand mask if one is handy. Repeat this four or five times, no more, and then take your hands away from your face. After a minute or so repeat this procedure if necessary. All the time try to stay calm and relaxed. Practice these techniques at times when you feel fine so that you will become expert for times that you may need them.

What To Do If You Are With Someone Who is Hyperventilating

1 Don't allow yourself to panic. Keep calm because fear can be infectious.
2 Familiarize yourself with each of the procedures described above. Encourage the person to use these procedures. They may need reminding of what to do, so it may help to talk them through it.
3 Don't shout or raise your voice. It should be firm but quiet. Speak slowly.
4 Comfort them physically – a hand gently cupping the back of their neck, or placing your arm loosely around their upper back may be very soothing.
5 They may become very emotional. Don't get into an argument by disagreeing with what they may be saying. Just repeat calming and encouraging statements, e.g., 'Just rebreathe your own air ... you're going to be all right ... that's it, just drop your shoulders ... relax'.
6 Afterwards treat as if for shock with rest and a sweet drink.

Overcoming the Effects of Chronic Hyperventilation

The procedures for rebreathing described are just as applicable to those who experience chronic symptoms of hyperventilation. It is important to find time for relaxation and generally winding down but also it may be helpful to 'rebreathe' four or five times a day to counteract any blowing off of carbon dioxide which may have occurred. Learn to notice patterns of sighing and yawning and take steps to alter patterns of breathing from the chest to the stomach, taking slow breaths six to eight per minute, breathing deeply to the bottom of the lungs. Practice breathing in this way for twenty minutes each day until it becomes second nature.

DISTRACTION

Why is Distraction Useful?

Thinking about unpleasant symptoms will tend to make them worse. It reminds us that we are feeling anxious and in doing so increases our fear that the symptoms may get worse as they have done in the past. We begin the 'fear of fear' cycle. This fear of fear will both provoke further symptoms as well as preventing the existing ones from diminishing naturally. This in turn produces worry, further fear of fear, which leads to yet further increase in symptoms by further turning on your stress tap. This vicious cycle is shown in Figure 5.2.

Figure 5.2   Fear of fear cycle

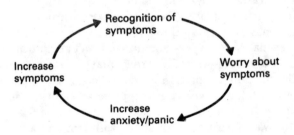

If, on the other hand, you do not let yourself pay attention to your symptoms, or worry about whether they are there or not, then it is less likely the vicious circle will be set up and so the symptoms will not get worse. Since the fear of fear will not be so great you will not be so distressed and then the anxiety will fade away of its own accord.

As you know it is very difficult just to turn your attention away from unpleasant feelings, especially since these feelings are a signal of stress. But you must learn to control these feelings by doing two things:

1 Be determined not to think about or dwell upon them.
2 Fill your mind with other things, distract yourself.

There are many techniques of distraction and it is very important that you practice with different methods to discover which one works best for you. Practice is important. Once the symptoms have begun we must act immediately, employing the specific technique of distraction which through practice we know works best for us.

Techniques of Distracting Yourself

Thought-Stopping Technique

This technique usually involves instruction from a therapist but may be learnt with practice and patience alone. Solo practice is a modification of the therapist's procedure as follows.

Basically you are asked to concentrate upon negative and troublesome thoughts and deliberately rehearse the thoughts out loud. As you gradually get more and more into the thoughts you suddenly shout 'STOP!' very loudly and clap your hands loudly simultaneously. Immediately you should find this loud noise has interrupted your train of thought, often enough to make you forget what it was that you were thinking about.

You must practice this technique many times until you find that every time you shout 'STOP!' the thoughts are successfully blocked. Remember to make a loud noise and vary the point in your thoughts at which you stop yourself.

After practising out loud the technique gradually shifts from speaking the thoughts to thinking them and shouting 'STOP!', then from there to thinking the thoughts and thinking the word 'STOP!'. Try and think of the word as just as shocking, just as loud, and you find, after practice, that it will stop your thoughts just as effectively in thought as out loud. Go through each of the stages about twenty times before moving on to the next stage. Practice several times daily until you become proficient.

Creating Mild Pain

The sensation of pain is a signal to the brain to act immediately to prevent the body from being hurt further. The signal of pain overrides any other signals that the brain may be receiving at that moment, any thoughts, ideas, or preoccupations are immediately swept aside so that the brain can attend to the pain and do something about it. Most of us can recall just how difficult it has been to concentrate on anything else if we have a headache or any other ache and pain.

The physiological and psychological mechanism by which pain can override all other signals is complex. Put simply, the brain is being constantly bombarded with signals from different sensory channels. Pain effectively closes the gate on all of these signals, they are shut out and the signal of pain is received. Therefore, one way of shutting off all negative and worrying thoughts, or shutting out any information to which we don't want to attend, is to create a mild sensation of pain for the brain to be occupied with.

Symptoms of anxiety may be controlled with practice using only a mild sensation of pain such as that created by digging your fingernails lightly into the palm of your hands, or pinching your earlobe, or gently biting your tongue or cheek. Another technique involves placing an elastic band on your wrist and gently twanging it in response to worrying irrational thoughts.

It is important obviously that you don't go too far with these techniques. Try different methods and use the one which works best for you. Certainly if you have to create anything other than mild pain in order to stop your thoughts you must not continue but rather find an alternative technique of distraction.

Like the thought-stopping procedures the creation of pain as a means of distraction is only a short term means of interrupting intense, worrying thoughts which occur repeatedly. You must then use these few seconds of relief from your negative thoughts to employ a more long term means of distraction to prevent the thoughts returning.

Attention Switching

In a sense all techniques of distraction are techniques of attention switching. We have however created this sub-heading for those techniques which offer more long term distraction than

106

those mentioned previously. There are very many ways of course to occupy the mind and the techniques we describe are only a few suggestions for practice. As before, successful attention switching depends upon careful preparation, having the techniques and the subjects to which to attend at our fingertips ready to distract us from negative or irrational thought.

Mantra techniques These techniques stem from transcendental meditation (TM) which is an extraction of eastern meditation systems. It requires no special lifestyle, just fifteen minutes quiet meditation using a 'mantra' two times each day. The mantra is a special word or sometimes a phrase given to the meditator by the TM instructor. The meditator is required to focus their mind upon the mantra in an effortless, relaxed way. Gradually as the person becomes more proficient, background noises and stimulation fade from attention, leaving the subject conscious and alert, but relaxed and calm.

This basic effect can be utilized for attention switching. Select any word or sentence, for instance the word 'calm' or 'my mind and body are calm'. Close your eyes and practice thinking it over and over again in your mind until you become proficient at blocking out all other thoughts and ideas, and can achieve a level of deep calm and relaxation. In this way heart rate, respiration rate, oxygen consumption, and muscle tension all reduce without conscious effort. Practice daily for fifteen or twenty minutes and you will then find that this word can be an effective means of blocking out unwanted thoughts and relaxing the body.

Environmental focus This refers to concentrating on and looking out for specific details in the world around you. An example might be to focus on car number plates and seeing if you can make a word containing all the letters of the plate number, or in a supermarket look out for all items costing a particular amount of money, or in a crowded room noting the number of people with blue eyes.

In this way the mind is busy and active. No opportunity is offered to rehearse any negative thoughts relating to how difficult a situation will be, or thoughts which focus on physical symptoms (and in doing so exacerbate these symptoms). Make up lots of things on which to focus the mind and start the process as soon as you set off, or start, whatever task you are attempting to achieve.

Use a 'bridging object'   A bridging object is one which carries you from your every day thoughts to happy memories in the past. A photo of a very happy holiday, a pebble or souvenir from a trip away, a ribbon from your wedding bouquet. Any photo or object which can instantly remind you of a particular event, place, or happy feeling can be used to switch your attention to focus on this pleasant scenario. Carry the item with you wherever you go and take it out and look at it to bring back these memories as a way of relaxing you, raising your spirits, and focusing your thoughts.

Mental games   Sometimes games which require concentrated thought can help distract you from your stress and anxiety. Buy a puzzle book and take it with you on long journeys in the car, or on public transport, or to use in your lunch hour at work. Games such as crosswords, mazes, find the hidden word, etc., can help prevent us from getting bored and allowing our thoughts to wander.

Another mental game which some people find effective is to try to think of a boy or girl's name for every letter of the alphabet, then an animal for every letter, and then an item in the kitchen, etc. Or if you are sitting in a room, look around you and see how many things there are more than two of. Other people use mathematical games to distract themselves such as adding continuously in threes, or counting backwards in sixes from 100, or learning and reciting poetry or a song. The actual nature of the game is not important so long as it focuses your attention effectively, distracting you from your negative thoughts or your symptoms. Don't try to think up games that are too difficult. They will only lead to frustration.

Behavioural activity   Keeping generally busy and active reduces the time available for brooding over problems. Plan ahead and get to know your vulnerable times when you are apt to have nothing to do and your mind begins to wander. How often do we switch on the television, only half watching it, or get stuck into routines in the evenings that require no conscious thought or effort, leaving the mind free to wander? Going for a walk, arranging to meet a friend, or just getting on with some DIY, hobby, or relaxation exercises are all likely to occupy the mind more effectively.

COGNITIVE-BEHAVIOURAL TECHNIQUES

Introduction

We present a summary of the main therapeutic techniques of three of the leading practitioners of cognitive therapy discussed in theoretical terms in chapter 2. Though you will note differences in the focus of their individual approach, as stated previously, all cognitive therapy techniques are based upon the premise that an individual's maladaptive behaviour is a function of distorted and irrational thinking and that altering these ways of thinking is an effective technique for changing behaviour. For a more extensive review of cognitive therapies the reader is referred to Dryden and Golden (1986).

The Techniques of Donald Meichenbaum

Self-instructional Methods

This approach to managing anxiety was devised by Meichenbaum (1975) and is based upon the idea that self-speech, the way we talk to ourselves, exerts control over our behaviour in much the same way as might speech coming from another person. Clients are often totally unaware of how negatively they may be talking to themselves, anticipating failure and minimizing success. The aim of the training is to help the individual to think more adaptively and to develop and improve their performance in any particular task. Basically these procedures attempt to teach the individual to talk to themselves in a confident and positive manner which anticipates success in the given task.

Clients are taught to initially monitor their self-statements in any chosen situation or task. They learn to then shift from negative, self-defeating internal dialogue towards positive, more realistic, and confidence-building self-speech. Tasks may be divided into three phases: preparation, coping, and praise. Each phase involves the clients saying a number of statements to themselves.

1 *Preparation for difficult situation*
    'It's not going to be as bad as I think'
    'I've coped with this very well before'
    'I might enjoy it if I try'
    'If I do get bad feelings I know they won't last long and that I will cope'
    'Avoiding the problem will make it worse I know I can face it'.
2 *Coping in the difficult situation*
    'This is just anxiety, I know it can't harm me'
    'Relax, thinking calming thoughts the feelings will go away'
    'In facing up to it, it won't beat me'
    'Be calm, concentrate on what I'm doing'
    'One step at a time, slowly does it'
3 *Praise following success in coping*
    'Great, well done, I coped'
    'I'm getting better, I'm in control'
    'I did that really well'
    'I handled it – it will be easier next time'

At each stage the client is encouraged to recite either one or a series of these statements. Initially this may be from a card containing the statements, but gradually the client will dispense with the cards as the statements come naturally.

Stress Inoculation Training (SIT)

These techniques are based upon the premise that anxiety results when a person perceives a discrepancy between the demands placed upon them and their personal resources for coping with those demands. (Lazarus 1966). Meichenbaum first developed these techniques in 1974 but they have recently been extended and detailed by Meichenbaum and Cameron (1983). The basic procedure is to provide the individual with as much information, and as many methods, as possible of handling stressful situations and reactions to them. This is detailed in three phases over many weeks of treatment as follows:

1 **Conceptualization:** a thorough assessment identifying
                            determinants of the problem,

110

	formulation of the problem and treatment plan, introduction of conceptual model and training the client to analyse problems independently.
2 Skills Acquisition and Rehearsal:	train in necessary skills, e.g., assertion, problem solving, distraction, relaxation, etc. Develop range of coping skills to assist flexible responses. Practise use of skills in role play. Teach self-instructional methods to develop mediators to regulate coping responses.
3 Application and follow through:	use of graded exposure to practise coping responses and build confidence. Role play use of techniques, different stressors practised, anticipated situations. Client coaches others. Develop strategies for recovering from failure. Arrange follow-ups.

The Techniques of Aaron Beck et al.

In their entirety the cognitive therapy techniques of Beck and his colleagues offer a complete system of psychotherapy. Only a broad outline of some of these methods is possible; the interested reader is referred to Beck and Emery (1985) for a more complete account. Therapy may be broken down into five basic stages or aspects.

Developing Awareness of Thought Processes.

Having offered the client a cognitive model for their anxiety problems, the therapist asserts the need to identify the thinking or images behind the anxiety. The therapist will initially focus on recent specific occurrences of anxiety symptoms and probe the client's recollection of their thoughts and fantasies. Often this will be written down, if possible in a sequential manner, helping the client realize how one negative or irrational image or thought can lead to another increasingly irrational thought at each stage. For example the lift phobic may say, 'I don't like lifts – I might get trapped – no one might notice – I'll be stuck there for ages – I'll begin to suffocate – I could be there for days – I'll starve to death.'

Once the person has understood what types of thoughts or images the therapist is looking for they are asked to keep a diary record of the daily occurrence of anxiety and related thoughts. The record form is a single sheet of paper as shown in Figure 5.3.

Figure 5.3   Recording automatic thoughts

Date/Time	Situation	Rating of Anxiety 1 –100	Automatic thoughts/ images
Tuesday 4	Shopping in local supermarket had panic attack	100	I'm going to faint, everyone will see, I can't even go shopping, I'm a failure.
Friday 5	Sitting watching television with company	80	This feeling of nausea is getting worse. I'm going to be sick. What if I can't get to the bathroom in time? What will our guests think?

Client Learns to Restructure Thinking/Imagery

The therapist asks the client three basic questions:

1 What's the evidence?
2 What's another way of looking at the situation?
3 So what if it happens?

The client is now helped to begin to challenge their irrational ideas and images and to aim towards a more logical and positive interpretation, by identifying what type of thinking error they are making. The double column technique may be used for this challenging process and to record further progress (see Figure 5.4).

Homework Target setting/Reality Testing

The client is encouraged, and initially assisted, in developing and carrying out strategies for testing thoughts and beliefs about what might happen, e.g. 'If I ask my boss for a raise he'll sack me

Figure 5.4 The double column technique

Automatic Thoughts/Images	Alternative Interpretation
I may have a panic attack and faint.	I've never fainted. If I control my breathing I'll cope like the last time.
I'll never get to the supermarket. I failed last time, I always fail.	Avoiding situations only makes things worse. If I control my panic as I've been taught I won't come to any harm. I will try. I've done it before. I can do it again.
No one will talk to me at the party. I'll be sat all alone, everyone will be laughing at me.	I know several people going and no one has ever laughed at me before. It's up to me to talk to them too. Staying in would only be worse, another night alone.

or bite my head off.', 'If I go to the cinema I'll have a panic attack and everyone will want to have me thrown out.'

Analyse Results of Reality Testing

Detailed analysis of the written account of the homework is carried out, with emphasis on reappraisal and re-attribution of original negative thoughts and beliefs. The client may be asked 'percentage belief', e.g. 'I was 100 per cent sure any girl would reject me'. The client's homework is to ring five girls to ask for a date. 'I'm only 50 per cent sure now, as two said they'd think about it'.

Use of Role Play

The client may be asked to swap roles with the therapist who expresses a number of negative irrational ideas which the client helps them to correct. Specific situations may also be role played prior to homework being conducted.

The Techniques of Albert Ellis

Rational Emotive Therapy (RET)

Ellis has written extensively about RET from 1962 onwards. For a more complete account of this field of work the reader is referred to Ellis and Grieger (1977), Dryden (1984). The task of the RET therapist is to identify, challenge, and thereby help the client to modify core irrational beliefs (see p. 41). This process occurs as a result of five stages, sometimes known as the ABCDE approach, which is illustrated with an example of a man whose girlfriend fails to turn up on their first date.

A = Activating Event
This refers to what actually happened – The girl failed to show up.
B = Beliefs both rational and irrational
These arise from the event – 'She doesn't like me ... I liked her ... She must like me ... she has to ... am I so awful? ... I'm unlikeable'.
C = Consequences
This refers to what the man's beliefs lead him to feel or do. He feels very upset, angry, and tense. He begins to doubt himself, lowering his self-confidence and self-esteem and making the next approach to a girl more difficult.
D = Disputing, Debating, Re-Defining
This is where therapy begins. Having identified the ABCs, the person's thoughts at point B are challenged. Assumptions are questioned, exaggerations tempered, and new and more rational alternatives are considered and discussed.
E = re-Evaluation toward a new Effect
Finally a new philosophy is established. The client expresses and believes in different, more rational interpretations – 'There is no rule which says somebody must love someone else, it would have been great if she'd turned up but there are other girls I could ask out. Because one person lets me down it doesn't mean I'm unloveable'.

Ellis would request that the client tests out his new hypothesis by ringing other girlfriends and arranging new dates. Identifying and challenging core irrational beliefs in this way becomes a life-long self-help strategy for the client, who gradually finds himself decreasingly prone to dysfunctional and automatic irrational thinking as RET itself becomes a way of life.

Chapter Six

HELPING CLIENTS TO CHANGE THEIR LIFESTYLES

INTRODUCTION

Learning to understand and manage symptoms of stress and anxiety helps the client to reduce the stress, they are under. However, alongside these measures, specifically directed towards the alleviation of symptoms, it is important to identify and change some of the external stresses that have caused the problems in the first place. These stresses may be exacerbated by the way the client organizes life at home and at work. They may be further exaggerated by the way the client communicates with others. The following chapter introduces a number of ideas and strategies for altering an individual's long-term behavioural patterns, or lifestyles. All of these strategies, education, specific self help skills, and life-style changes, aim to reduce stress by turning off the stress tap and draining the stress glass.

GOAL PLANNING

The Importance of Goals

Life may be construed as a series of ever growing accomplishments as we move towards a multitude of personal goals. Achieving these goals is a key to high self-esteem, happiness and peak performance. People who are unhappy are often people who do not have goals. Without goals to strive for our lives can become empty, meaningless, and stressful. Some people are more aware of the goals they are working towards than others and subsequently have a greater sense of direction and purpose. In studies of survivors of the horrors of prison camps, those who had a purpose in living, with well defined goals, were able to withstand greater deprivation such as starvation and torture. The purpose for living could have been revenge, to build a new homeland, or to see their family. Prisoners flexible enough to develop new goals also seem to cope better, even if those goals were something along the lines of becoming the world record holder for the number of consecutive push ups. A more contemporary example is the man who finally retires after a lifetime of work, with no new goals or plans. The emptiness can be devastating and very stressful. Recent research provides further examples. In one study a random group of residents in a home for the elderly and infirm were given a house plant to own and look after. Results indicated that the 'houseplant group' lived significantly longer than a matched control group, perhaps simply because the plants gave them some extra purpose in life.

Goal planning is the act of deciding what you really want to do and then how you will go about doing it. The goal is made concrete by writing it down and making a commitment to it. Obstacles on the way to that goal must be anticipated, identified, and viewed as challenges. There are of course reasons why people do not set goals: they may not realize the importance of goals; they may not know how to set about it; or more importantly, they may have a fear of failure. Thomas Edison, the man who eventually invented the electric light bulb, said 'failure is essential to success ... you cannot succeed without failing ... double your failure rate if you want to succeed.'

Planning our future gives us a greater sense of internal control and increases self-esteem. Being able to anticipate the demands of the future makes us less vulnerable to stress. The method of goal planning we will present here may be particularly helpful for clients with stress related problems. The exercise consists of three steps:

1 The selection of goals
2 Deriving objectives from goals
3 Selecting activities for the achievement of objectives

The Selection of Goals

Ask yourself the question 'What do I want out of life?' Start answering the question in terms of broad, general categories. Be imaginative, brainstorm yourself, writing down all the ideas that come into your head. Think about all the things you would like to achieve, obtain, or experience, within the next five years, in different areas of your life – work, home, leisure, personal – and then list them. Include anything you feel you want even if it's not realistic or sensible. A list from one of our clients had these items (not in order of priorities):

Home
1 To live in a nice house
2 To have a wife and children
Work
3 To get promoted
4 To get some research published
Personal
5 To travel around the world
6 To have an affair with Meryl Streep
7 To find peace within myself
8 To have a circle of good friends
Leisure
9 To beat Boris Becker at tennis
10 To create a work of art

Once you have generated the list go back and examine it in the following fashion:

(a) Look first for goals that are not within your power to achieve: from the above list, 6 and 9 are low probability items – impossible to achieve for most of us. Spending a great deal of time trying to achieve these goals will be unproductive and frustrating. It would be like betting a large sum of money on a million to one shot. Goals like a tennis victory over Boris Becker can, however, be changed to achievable ones, such as, improving your game of tennis. If modifying the goal to make it achievable turns it into something you no longer care about, then drop the goal altogether.

(b) Try to make each goal as clear and specific as possible. The clearer a goal is, the easier it is to decide whether the goal is attainable, and if it is attainable, how you would go about achieving it. For example, on reflection, item 7 was changed to 'being able to relax and unwind after work and at weekends'.

(c) Look for inconsistencies among your goals. Working

117

towards imcompatible goals can cause a great deal of psycho-logical stress. Nobody can function effectively when attempting to move simultaneously in opposite directions. Examples of some pairs of goals that are inconsistent in all but the rarest cases are: 'have children' and also 'have a great deal of freedom'; 'rise to the top of your profession' and 'never work weekends or evenings'; 'have strong opinions, speak your mind,' and 'still have everybody like you'. Finding incompatible goals may cause you to drop one or more from your list, or reduce the import-ance of some goals. At the very least, spotting conflicting goals will alert you to potential problems.

(d) Decide which goals are most important to you. Rank order them.

Deriving Objectives from Goals

Once you have analyzed and redefined your list of goals, you are ready to derive a set of objectives for each of your goals. Objectives are specific, concrete outcomes, that further your progress towards a goal. A statement of an objective must always refer to some publicly observable outcome occurring within a certain time frame. For example, the goal 'to create a work of art', has the objective, 'to write a 10,000 word short story by the end of the year'. The goal of 'achieving wealth', has the objec-tive, 'to be achieving an income of £20,000 as head of my own department, within the next three years'.

Objectives perform an important function. They enable us to break up the larger and more nebulous goals, into smaller, more manageable pieces. They also help us keep tabs on our progress.

Selecting Activities for the Achievement of Objectives

Once you have clear precise objectives you will be ready to select activities for the achievement of each objective. Well stated objectives often suggest the activity necessary to accomplish them. Activities are the specific behaviour that leads towards achieving objectives. Activities that would lead towards the objective of writing a short story might be, 'clear the spare room out and set up a desk', 'enroll on a weekend workshop on creative writing', 'set aside the next four Sunday afternoons for writing', 'arrange to visit a friend in six weeks' time with a completed first draft'. Activities that might lead to the objective of promotion to head of a department might be, 'enroll on a management course', 'achieve at least four research publications within the next two years', 'join two committees and get involved with service planning'.

TIME MANAGEMENT

Sharper Not Harder

Once a person has established goals and activities, and has time-tabled these projects in terms of dates of achievement, the effective management of time becomes important. This does not mean that the person needs necessarily to go faster, but that they organize their time more effectively.

Charlesworth and Nathan (1982) tell a very poignant story about a young man who always wanted to be a lumberjack. He wandered up to the logging camp on his eighteenth birthday and enthusiastically asked for a job. Seeing that the boy was large, strong, and healthy, the boss quickly agreed. The first day the lad chopped down ten large trees entirely by himself. This was quite an accomplishment and the boss was very pleased. The next day the boy seemed to work just as hard and just as long, but he only chopped down eight trees. This was still quite respectable. The rest of the week passed and each day the boy worked just as hard and just as long, but each day he produced less. On Friday the boss called the boy into his office noticing that he had only felled one tree. He was ashamed because he had produced so little and tears began to roll down his face.

'Sir' he said, 'I'm working harder and harder, but I'm afraid I'm disappointing you'. 'Why do you do so little?' the boss asked. 'I'm really trying sir,' was the boy's response. 'Have you taken time to sharpen your axe, boy?' enquired the boss. The boy answered, 'No sir, I really haven't had time because I've been so busy working.' The moral: work sharper, not harder.

The lesson to be learned is that taking time out of a fixed routine to stand back, and reassess the situation, is time well spent, and can create greater efficiency and productivity.

Taking Breaks to Increase Productivity

Productivity increases as we spend more time and energy, but only up to a critical point. Past that point the productivity curve decreases. For example if studying for an exam, it is well established that studying for long periods without a break is literally, a waste of time. The human brain, particularly memory, works best for concentrated periods of about forty to fifty minutes. Then after this time, a short ten to fifteen minutes break provides primary and recovery effects and helps consolidate previously learned material. The student or executive who sits down and works non stop for two to three hours is not using their time productively, as, after fifty minutes, memory, concentration, and attentional skills decline. A ten minute tea-break, a telephone call, a brief conversation, anything which breaks up large blocks of concentration, improves efficiency. Deliberately changing tasks from writing to talking re-channels our mental energies, providing a break from one particular mental style, which again increases productivity. Working through a lunch-break is usually not a very good idea. Even a twenty minute walk across the park, and a sandwich in the fresh air, is an effective way of using time productively.

Similarly, after a week of hard stressful work, it is important to schedule relaxing and distracting activities for the weekend. Having a relaxing hobby or interest, which takes us physically and mentally away from work can be an invaluable insulator against a build-up of stress. It seems to help if the leisure activity is opposite in as many ways as possible from the work situation. For example if you work indoors, at a desk, doing clerical work, a suitable hobby might involve being outside, doing some physical activity. Holidays can also be a valuable source of relaxation and distraction.

Lists and Priorities

Taking five minutes in the morning, at the beginning of the day, to draw up a 'things to do' list is a useful way of planning time. If large goals are broken down into small specified short-term tasks, a sense of purpose is created. Meeting these attainable short-term goals and progressively crossing them off the list can provide an important sense of achievement and reinforcement.

Making a list also offers the opportunity to set priorities, assessing which tasks have to be achieved, which tasks can wait, and which tasks can be delegated. A helpful strategy is to rate tasks in terms of A, B, or C priorities; where A is 'At once', B is 'Best done today', and C is 'Can wait'. Spending large amounts of time on 'C' items at the expense of 'A' items is unproductive.

An eighteenth century economist named Pareto suggested the 'Pareto Principle' or the '80/20 rule'. Simply stated, only 20 per cent of the tasks we do in a day produce 80 per cent of the rewards. Remembering this principle will help you to concentrate your energies on the right 20 per cent of tasks, making these the 'A' priorities. It will also help you to become more comfortable with not doing 'C' items.

The perfectionist is a person who has problems setting priorities, and often ends up spending equal amounts of time and effort on tasks irrespective of their importance. Perfectionists end up working slowly, doing everything very well, putting themselves under pressure. It is useful for such people to learn to vary the quality of their effort. This might involve deliberately doing something quickly and poorly. Attempting to do everything perfectly can lead to doing everything adequately, but nothing exceptionally.

Problem Solving and Making Decisions

Some people have great difficulty in solving problems and making decisions and waste a great deal of time ruminating on the same thoughts without ever coming to a clear conclusion. In these situations help is needed to organize thoughts and separate 'the wood from the trees'. The following exercises can be useful to make conscious, clarify, and hopefully resolve finely balanced internal debates.

Exercise 1: Decision-Making

Take a sheet of paper and at the top write the decision at issue. Draw a line down the middle from top to bottom. Head the left-hand column 'reasons for' and write down all the reasons you can think of to follow a particular choice. Similarly head the right-hand column 'reasons against', and write down all the reasons as to why you should not make that choice. The choice is now clearer as your thoughts are visible, being on paper (see Figure 6.1).

If still unable to make a decision, weigh the 'pros' and 'cons' in terms of importance. Assign a rating on a ten-point scale as to how important each consideration is.

If a choice is still problematic, put the piece of paper in a drawer and come back to it the next day.

Figure 6.1 Example of decision-making – changing job

REASONS FOR CHANGING JOB	REASONS AGAINST CHANGING JOB
1 A good career move – look good on my C.V.	1 New job will restrict my freedom. Will not have so much time to write book.
2 More money.	2 New job will involve a great deal of travelling.
3 A challenge and an interesting new area to work in.	3 I am content with present job. I'm still learning and there are still plenty of challenges to meet.
4 Opportunity to meet new people.	4 New job will entail a house move to an area where property prices are not increasing as much. It will be difficult to move south again.
5 Be able to buy a bigger house.	5 Moving will involve leaving a comfortable circle of friends and social activities.
6 Would be close to family.	6 I like this area because the countryside is pretty and it is close to lively and varied cultural centres.
7 I've been in this company for six years now – I don't want to get stuck.	

Exercise 2: Problem Solving

Identify the problem, e.g. should I go on holiday to Australia to meet a friend – I don't know if I can afford it?

Try to list all the possible options without thinking about them too closely. Brainstorm yourself, generating as many options as possible – just write down any option that comes into your head irrespective of how realistic or unrealistic:

1 I could borrow money to go.
2 I could work overtime to raise the money.
3 If I didn't go I could stay at home and work on the house.
4 If I didn't go, I could have a summer holiday in Greece and still afford a skiing holiday in winter.
5 I could visit my sister in Weymouth and buy a new car with the saved money.
6 We could arrange to meet halfway, say, Thailand or India. The flight and cost of living would be less expensive in a third-world country.
7 I could stay at home and try to write a novel.
8 I could go around the country visiting old friends and relatives.

Look at each option carefully and consider the likely consequences of each course of action. Decide which options are unrealistic and exclude them, for example:

> I cannot borrow that amount of money because I'm already overdrawn and I don't know anybody who would lend me any.
>
> I could not face the prospect of spending a long holiday in Weymouth, because I would argue with my sister, and it rains too much in Weymouth. I want the sun.
>
> I could not stay at home and write a novel because I feel too tired and run down, and need a break from mental activity.

Select from the remaining options. Make a decision as to which option would be most rewarding and feasible. If necessary use the decision-making exercise to weigh up the pros and cons of closely competing options as described previously.

Prepare and plan strategy for accomplishment of chosen option.

BEING MORE ASSERTIVE

What is Assertiveness Training?

The way we behave and communicate with others at work, home, or in public, can be an important factor in the development of stress. Poor communication can lead to unhealthy relationships, and unhealthy relationships are likely to increase stress. At the heart of healthy interpersonal communication is the skill of assertiveness. Individuals with poor assertiveness skills create a variety of problems for themselves. For example, the person who cannot say 'no' to others' requests is likely to be overwhelmed by external demands; the person who fails to speak up for him/herself and express personal feelings and thoughts will not feel fulfilled and comfortable with his/her own identity; the person who can communicate only in an aggressive manner may fail to develop healthy trusting relationships. Communication skills affect every area of life, from expressing feelings in intimate relationships to dealing with over-zealous shop assistants.

Assertiveness training is a structured form of intervention aimed at improving the effectiveness of our communication style. The approach is not restricted to a clinical population, but has been used extensively in the commercial world particularly in the fields of sales and management.

An assertiveness training programme involves a number of stages: first, understanding the underlying principles of the approach; second, recognizing different styles of communicating (passive, aggressive, assertive), third, identifying specific situations where we would like to be more assertive, whether at work, in public, among friends, or at home; fourth, to prepare, rehearse, or role play a different, more assertive response; and fifth, to transfer that behaviour back into the real world.

The Philosophy of Assertiveness Training

The underlying philosophy of assertiveness training is based on the premise that we are all equal; nobody is more important or less important than anybody else. Because we are all equal, we all possess the same basic human rights. The goal of assertiveness should be to stand up for one's rights without violating the rights of others. A good starting point for any assertiveness training is to remind ourselves of some of these basic rights (see Figure 6.2).

Any one of the rights on the list can be personalized. For example, the stressed housewife may take rights 3 and 7 and decide that: 'I have the right to suggest to my elderly mother-in-law that she enquire about the possibility of a home-help, as the demands she is making on me are wearing me out'.

124

Figure 6.2 Our rights

1 I have the right to express my feelings.
2 I have the right to express my opinions and beliefs.
3 I have the right to say 'Yes' and 'No' for myself.
4 I have the right to change my mind.
5 I have the right to say, 'I don't understand'.
6 I have the right to simply be myself without having to act for other people's benefit.
7 I have the right to decline responsibility for other people's problems.
8 I have the right to make reasonable requests of others.
9 I have the right to set my own priorities.
10 I have the right to be listened to, and taken seriously.
Add your own:

Communication Styles Passive/Aggressive/Assertive

We all display different degrees of passive, aggressive, or assertive behaviour, at different times, in different situations. Problems arise when we get stuck in a particular style of response which is unhelpful and find changing to a more appropriate style of response difficult. Assertiveness training is about extending and being flexible in our communication style so that we have more choices as to how we respond in different situations. The three categories of passive, aggressive and assertive behaviour are a useful way of differentiating and describing interpersonal communication styles.

Passive Behaviour

This involves violating one's own rights by failing to express honest feelings, thoughts and beliefs, and consequently permitting others to violate oneself. Passive or non-assertive behaviour can also mean expressing one's thoughts and feelings in such an apologetic and self-effacing manner that others can easily disregard them. The passive responder allows others to 'walk all over them' (doormat). The non-assertive person feels they have no control over their anxiety: it controls and immobilizes them. The passive person does not allow their needs to take precedence over or be as valid as, another's. They allow others to make their decisions for them, even though they may resent it later. They feel helpless, powerless, and inhibited. Non-assertion

125

shows a subtle lack of respect for the other person's ability to take disappointments, to shoulder some responsibility, to handle their own problems.

Message communicated   I don't count, so you can take advantage of me. My feelings, needs, and thoughts are less important than yours. I'll put up with just about anything from you. I'm not OK – you're OK.

Subliminal thoughts   Take care of me and understand my needs magically. Will you still love/respect me if I am assertive? I've got to protect you from hurt.

Goal   To appease others and to avoid conflict and unpleasantness at any cost.

Verbal and non-verbal characteristics

Rambling – letting things slide without comment.
Beating around the bush – not saying what you mean.
Apologizing inappropriately – soft, unsteady voice.
Being unclear – averted gaze.
Posture – backs off from others – slouched shoulders.
Wringing hands – winks or laughs when expressing anger.
Covering mouth with hand.
'... if it wouldn't be too much trouble'.
'but do whatever you want'.
'I ... er ... um ... would like ... um ... you ... er ... to do ...'.

Payoffs   You are praised for being selfless, a good sport. If things go wrong, as a passive follower, you are rarely blamed. Others will protect and look after you. You avoid, postpone, or hide the conflict that you fear.

Price   Others often make unreasonable demands on you. When, by your lack of assertion, you have allowed a relationship to develop in a way you don't like, shifting the pattern becomes more difficult. You crowd yourself into other people's images of a lovable, good person. When you repress or bottle up so much anger, you simultaneously diminish other feelings, including love and affection.

Aggressive Behaviour

This involves standing up for one's personal rights and expressing one's thoughts, feelings, and beliefs in a way which is usually inappropriate and always violates the rights of the other person. People often feel devastated by an encounter with an aggressive person. Superiority is maintained by putting others down. When threatened, you attack, aiming at the vulnerability exposed in the other.

Message communicated   This is what I think, what I want, what I feel. What matters to you isn't important to me. 'I'm OK – you're not OK'.

Subliminal thoughts   'I'll get you, before you have a chance of getting me'. 'I'm out for Number One'.

Goal   Domination, winning, forcing the other person to lose, punishing.

Verbal and non-verbal characteristics

   Body leans over the other's space intrusively.
   Staring the other person down.
   Strident voice.
   Sarcastic or condescending voice.
   Chilling cold and detached voice.
   Parental body gestures (finger pointing).
   Threats ('You'd better watch out ...', 'If you don't ...').
   Put downs ('You've got to be kidding', 'Don't be so stupid').
   Evaluative comments ('should', 'bad', 'ought').
   Sexist/racist remarks.

Pay offs   You get others to do your bidding. Things tend to go your way and you like that feeling of control in shaping your life. You are likely to secure the material needs and objects you desire. You are less vulnerable in a culture characterized by struggle, hostility, and competition.

Price   Aggressive behaviour creates enemies, which can induce greater fear and a sense of paranoia, making it difficult for you to relax. If, through your aggression, you control what I do, it takes your time and energy to supervise me, thus creating a paradoxical self-imposed servitude. You become alienated from others.

Assertive Behaviour

This involves standing up for personal rights and expressing your thoughts, feelings, and beliefs directly, honestly, and spontaneously in ways that are respectful of the rights of others. An assertive person evaluates a situation, decides how to act, and responds without undue anxiety or guilt. Assertive people respect themselves and other people and take responsibility for their actions and choices. They recognize their needs and ask openly and directly for what they want. If refused, they may feel saddened, disappointed, or inconvenienced, but their self-concept isn't shattered. They are not reliant on the approval of others, and anchor their supports deeply within themselves as well as externally. Assertive people teach other people how they wish to be treated.

Message communicated   This is what I think. This is how I feel. This is how I see the situation. How about you? 'I'm OK – you're OK'. If our needs conflict I am certainly ready to explore our differences and I may be prepared to compromise.

Subliminal thoughts   I won't allow you to take advantage of me and I won't attack you for being who you are.

Verbal and non-verbal characteristics

General demeanour suggests assurance, caring, and understanding.
Receptive listening.
Firm, relaxed voice.
Direct eye contact.
Erect, balanced, open body stance.
Voice appropriately loud to the situation.
'I' statements ('I like', 'I want', 'I don't like').
Co-operative phrases ('How can we resolve this?', 'What are your thoughts on this?')
Emphatic statements of interest ('I would like to work on this project')

Pay offs The more you stand up for yourself and act in a manner you respect, the higher your self-esteem. Your chances of getting what you want out of life improve greatly when you let others know what you want and stand up for your own rights and needs. Expressing yourself at the time of negative feelings means you will be less apt to hurt someone. Resentment has not built up and feelings are typically at a low level of distress. Being less preoccupied with self-consciousness and anxiety, and less driven by the needs of self-protection and control, you can see, hear, and love others more easily.

Price Because you are not assertive in a vacuum, assertion can disrupt your relationships. Your family/spouse/colleagues/friends may have benefitted from your non-assertion and may sabotage your newly developed assertion. There is pain involved in developing honest, caring confrontations. You are re-shaping your beliefs and re-examining your values that have been closely held since childhood. This can be frightening. You must confront your fears and doubts and take risks again and again. There is no 'Tablet from the Mount' to guarantee an elegant outcome of your efforts.

Identifying Situations to Work On

The next stage in an assertiveness programme involves identifying particular situations or activities where the client could be more assertive. The 'Rating Your Assertiveness Chart', and the 'Everyday Situations that may require Assertiveness' lists provide a useful outline and examples of the different activities that make up assertive behaviour (see Figures 6.3 and 6.4).

It is important then to draw up a list of specific personal examples which create difficulties for the client. Each situation on the list should then be rated on a score out of ten, and arranged in terms of difficulty. Situations should then be rated in order, with the most difficult at the top and the easiest at the bottom, in the same manner as the hierarchical approach discussed in chapter 4 (see Figure 6.5).

Figure 6.3   Everyday situations that may require assertiveness

AT WORK
How do you respond when:
1 You receive a compliment on your appearance, or someone praises your work?
2 You are criticized unfairly?
3 You are criticized legitimately by a superior?
4 You have to confront a subordinate for continual lateness or sloppy work?
5 Your boss makes a sexual innuendo, or makes a pass at you?

IN PUBLIC
How do you respond when:
1 In a restaurant the food you ordered arrives cold or overcooked?
2 A fellow passenger in a no smoking compartment lights a cigarette?
3 You are faced with an unhelpful shop assistant?
4 Sombody barges in front of you in a queue?
5 You take an inferior article back to a shop?

AMONGST FRIENDS
How do you respond when:
1 You feel angry with the way a friend has treated you?
2 A friend makes what you consider to be an unreasonable request?
3 You want to ask a friend for a favour?
4 You ask a friend for repayment of a loan of money?
5 You have to negotiate with a friend on which film to see or where to meet?

AT HOME
How do you respond when:
1 One of your parents criticizes you?
2 You are irritated by a persistant habit in someone you love?
3 Everybody leaves the washing-up to you?
4 You want to say 'No' to a proposed visit to a relative?
5 Your partner feels amorous but you are not in the mood?

Responding Differently

The fifth step in an assertiveness programme involves preparing and rehearsing a different way of responding to the identified situation. This involves discussing how the client could respond differently and looking at specific verbal and non-verbal characteristics of an assertive response. The client might then be asked to close their eyes and visualize how they might respond differently, or to role play the new behaviour with the therapist. Video feedback has also been used effectively in these types of training programmes. To lighten what can be quite an anxiety provoking

Figure 6.4 Rating your assertiveness

DIRECTIONS: Fill in each block with a rating of your assertiveness on a 5-point scale. A rating of 0 means you have no difficulty asserting yourself. A rating of 5 means you are completely unable to assert yourself.

PEOPLE / ACTIVITY	Friends of the same sex	Friends of different sex	Intimate relations or spouse	Authority figures	Relatives, Family members	Colleagues and subordinates	Strangers	Service workers waiters, shop assistants, etc.
Giving compliments								
Make requests, e.g. ask for favours/help								
Initiate and maintain conversation								
Refuse requests								
Express personal opinions								
Express anger/ displeasure								
Express liking, love, affection								
Stating your rights and needs								

Figure 6.5 Example of a personal list of assertiveness situations to work on

1 Telling my boss that I don't want to work on Saturday mornings.	9/10
2 Delegate the Monroe account to Harry Spencer.	8/10
3 Refuse Jim's request next time he asks for a loan.	7/10
4 Ask mother-in-law not to smoke in my house.	7/10
5 Return those uncomfortable shoes to the shop.	6/10
6 Tell Helen that she's doing a really good job.	5/10
7 Invite the neighbour over for a drink.	5/10
8 Give Dad a hug next time I greet him.	4/10
9 Ask Peter to return the record he borrowed last year.	3/10
10 Ask the neighbour if they would feed the cat this weekend.	2/10

experience, it is sometimes helpful to ask the client to role play a particular situation, but to do it at first, extremely badly. So, the unassertive client can role play being even more unassertive than they really are, and then role play being gradually more assertive. Assertiveness training can be fun as well as being an effective way of changing behaviour. A number of key verbal and non-verbal assertive skills to remember include:

1 Establish good eye contact but do not stare.
2 Stand or sit comfortably without fidgeting.
3 Talk in a firm steady voice rather than shouting or rambling.
4 Use gesture to emphasize points (hands, facial expressions, body posture).
5 Use statements such as 'I think', 'I feel'.
6 Use co-operative words such as 'let's' or 'we could'.
7 Use empathic statements of interest such as 'What do you think', 'How do you feel?'
8 Be concise and to the point. Clearly state the message you want the other person to hear. If necessary use the 'broken record technique' – repeating the core message over and over again. Keep problem centred and don't be side-tracked by personal attacks or distractions.

Transferring Back to the Real World

After the relative safety of role playing either with a thera-pist alone, or in a group, or merely imaging how to behave differently, comes the transfer or generalization of training. It is useful for the client to set him/herself specific homework assignments to complete before the following session – the notion of reporting back to one person, or a group, acts as an incentive for action. Again the simple principle is to start with easier tasks and progress to more difficult ones. Confidence develops through the accumulation of successes. Aim for smaller success to start off with, rather than taking too large a leap which might result in disappointment and reduction in confidence.

For more details of assertiveness training see Smith (1975), Dickson (1982), and Alberti and Emmons (1970).

MANAGING TYPE-A BEHAVIOUR

As discussed in chapter 1, high scorers on Type-A behaviour inventories – people with 'hurry sickness' – are more susceptible to symptoms of anxiety, and stress induced illnesses. However, research suggests that most successful and satisfied executives show classic Type-A behaviours. Friedman and Rosenman (1974) suggest that it is not a question of getting rid of Type-A behaviour, rather that we should learn to manage it. They make a number of suggestions, or 'drills against hurry sickness'. After a client has completed the Type-A inventory, and identified areas for possible change, the following drills may be useful. The therapist will be deliberately encouraging the client to 'go against the grain', by negotiating specific behavioural homework tasks.

Try to restrain from being the centre of attention by constantly talking. Force yourself to LISTEN to other people. Stop finishing sentences for other people. Ask yourself the question 'Do I really have anything important to say?' and 'Does anyone want to hear it?' Search out somebody that talks slowly, and deliberately have a slow conversation.

Try to control your obsessional, time-directed life by making yourself more aware of it, and changing the established pattern of behaviour. Whenever you catch yourself speeding up in a car to get through a red light, deliberately penalize yourself by turning right at the next corner. Circle the road and approach the same signal again. Similarly, deliberately walk slowly and set yourself a specific time period for a relaxing lunchbreak. See how long you can take to eat a meal or a sandwich, chewing every mouthful as slowly as possible.

Take as many stressfree 'breathing spaces' during the course of an intensive work day as possible. Make sure you do something that relaxes you; it can mean reading the newspaper, taking a walk, talking to people you like, etc. Include five-minute intense relaxation spots during both morning and afternoon, where you concentrate on relaxing muscles, slowing your breathing down and calming your mind.

Take time out to assess the cause of your 'hurry sickness' and 'hostility'. Is it due to a need to feel important? Is it designed to avoid some activity or person? Is this hostility the result of feeling threatened and insecure about the present situation?

Make a deliberate effort to develop enjoyable leisure activities and hobbies. Look back on the activities you have enjoyed in the past and select one to develop. Commit yourself fully to participate in such activities. Don't allow all your energy to be channelled into work.

Try not to bottle up emotions. Ventilate your feelings. Talk to others about your problems and about how you feel. Allow yourself opportunities to express anger, frustration, and sadness. A problem shared is a problem halved.

INCREASE YOUR SOCIAL SUPPORT NETWORK

There is substantial evidence that social support, at work or at home, may provide an effective insulator or buffer against the effects of stress. A number of studies (Marmot 1975 and others) have shown markedly reduced rates of coronary heart disease in Japan compared to the United States. This seems to be related to certain features of Japanese lifestyle and working practices, such as shared decision-making, group affiliations, corporate identity, group counselling, etc. Other research has shown that women with a confiding relationship are much less likely to become depressed.

Many clients falsely assume that an extensive social network, involving family, friends and colleagues, just happens. This is blatantly untrue. The maintenance of friendships and relationships requires a certain amount of deliberate effort and hard work: they have to be developed and cultivated. The overall goal of 'increasing social contacts', just like 'having more money', can be broken down into specific objectives and activities. Homework tasks may centre around the client achieving specific behavioural tasks. Examples of these tasks include, 'chatting for two minutes to the man in the corner shop', 'inviting the neighbour around for a drink', 'enrolling in an evening class', 'joining a club or society', 'telephoning an old friend', etc. These homework tasks are negotiated between therapist and client. It is important not to take on over-ambitious tasks or the client will feel demoralized. Small achievable tasks increase confidence, leading to more difficult tasks. The underlying principle of such homework tasks, in the form of self-help therapy, is that everybody can set themselves a task, however small, and achieve it.

A professional mental health worker should have access to information concerning local support and self-help groups. These groups might range from mother and toddler groups, to specific self-help groups like Alcoholics Anonymous, Weight Watchers, or Open Door. We would see it as part of the role of the mental health worker to encourage and support the development of such groups. Self-help groups can be developed by interested clients who have completed structured anxiety management courses. Group-based therapies like anxiety management groups have the added ingredient of offering clients an additional social network of others with similar difficulties. Our research has indicated that clients find this 'meeting others in the same boat' one of the most helpful components of therapy.

A HEALTHIER LIFESTYLE

Physical Exercise

A healthy, strong body copes better with stressful situations and is a means, like relaxation, of draining the stress glass. The 600 muscles in our body thrive on exercise and deteriorate without it. Regular exercise produces a number of benefits:

1 Exercise provides a way of releasing a great deal of the muscle tension, and general physical arousal (adrenalin) accumulated in the body's response to stress. An important benefit of exercise is muscle relaxation.

2 Exercise helps develop and maintain good circulation and lowers blood pressure.

3 Exercise improves immunization in the body's constant fight to ward off disease.

4 Exercise can be used to clear the mind of the clutter of worrying thoughts and anxieties. Often more creative ideas and more effective problem solving occur after exercise.

5 Exercise improves self-image, appearance, and control of weight.

6 Research has shown that hormones are relased during exercise which act as natural anti-depressants (endomorphines).

Getting Fitter

Ideally exercise for general fitness should involve as many of the body muscles as possible. Getting fit is about small amounts of physical exercise, starting slowly and gradually building up a regular routine. There are three aspects to fitness: stamina, suppleness, and strength.

Stamina It is the heart and lungs which provide a person with stamina. Any exercises which increase the body's need for oxygen will be exercising the heart and lungs. These specific types of exercise are called aerobic exercises. The heart is a muscle and, just like any other in the body, it can become unfit. Toning up the heart and lungs leads to a more effective supply of oxygen to the blood which in turn is supplied more quickly to the muscles, enabling us to stave off exhaustion.

Suppleness Exercises ranging from yoga to vigorous swimming engage the body's muscles in regular and rhythmic movements. This reduces stiffness, enables the person to move more freely, and will serve to reduce arthritic problems in elderly people.

Strength This stems in part from both stamina and suppleness. Most of us do not really aspire to developing huge muscles, enabling us to lift great weights, but, by developing extra strength, the muscles are then working well within their capability for most everyday tasks. The therapist can encourage the client to introduce regular exercise into their weekly schedule. Specific behavioural targets can be negotiated. These might be to: 'go swimming for thirty minutes after work once a week', 'use the stairs rather than the lift', 'walk to the restaurant instead of driving'.

Nutrition and Weight Control

People respond to stress in different ways, some smoke, some drink alcohol, and some increase and decrease their food consumption. All these behaviours are part of a vicious circle where a maladaptive response to stress produces more stress. Consider the example of overeating. The effect of overeating is weight gain, which in itself is an added stress. A person 25 per cent over their normal weight range has a two and a half times greater chance of having a heart attack, hypertension, or a stroke. The overweight person's self-image may also fall, causing a loss of confidence, which becomes another stress.

A healthy well-balanced diet containing proper nutrition can be used to help cope with stress. People who eat properly feel good about themselves. The following dietary guideline can be woven into therapy if it appears that the client has an unhealthy diet.

1 Avoid too much fat, saturated fat, and cholesterol – grill, bake, or boil rather than frying.
2 Eat foods with adequate starch or fibre (roughage) e.g., bran, wholemeal bread, fresh vegetables and fruits.
3 Avoid too much sugar. Try doing without sugar in beverages or use a tablet or liquid sweetener.
4 Avoid too much salt. Do not automatically add salt to a meal. Avoid savoury manufactured goods and crisps.
5 Eat a variety of foods including fresh ones. In this way you should receive all the nourishment, minerals, and vitamins you need.
6 Attempt to maintain your ideal body weight.
7 Avoid excessive amounts of caffeine (in coffee, tea, Cola drinks), especially before sleeping, as it is a stimulant which has a direct effect on the nervous system.
8 The recommended maximum weekly intake of alcohol is twenty-one units for men and fourteen units for women. One unit is equivalent to one pub measure or glass of wine, sherry,

or whisky, or half a pint of beer or cider. When taken in excess alcohol causes liver damage, blood sugar problems, impaired brain function, and induces dependence.

9 There is no doubt that smoking is damaging to your health and impairs long term ability to cope with stress. It is estimated that for every cigarette you smoke you shorten your life span by five minutes.

Sleeping Difficulties

For all of us getting a good night's deep sleep is important. Sleep provides a restorative function within the body, slowing down bodily processes, and providing a much needed break from daily stress. The pattern and exact nature of sleep that we get will vary enormously from one individual to another. Some people can get by on three or four hours a night whilst others seem to need much more. It is very important to realize that the body regulates itself very effectively in terms of its sleep requirements. Though it is very disconcerting when we find we can't drop off or that we wake early, we must remember that we cannot do ourselves any physical harm by having difficulty sleeping. Though we may become more irritable and find life's demands more stressful, loss of sleep is not physically damaging to the body.

Basically there are five stages to sleep. Stages 1 and 2 are stages of light sleep, just drifting off and being asleep but easily aroused. Stages 3 and 4 are the deep stages of sleep. It is those stages that provide the real 'quality' sleep. The shorter the length of time we are asleep the more the body will adjust so that sleep will be spent in these deeper phases. This is why less sleep can be just as effective in restoring us physically, though we may be used to sleeping longer. The fifth stage of sleep is known as REM (Rapid Eye Movement) sleep. It is during this fifth stage that we dream. Again there is marked variation from one person to another and from one week to another in the amount of dream sleep that we get. Different theorists offer different explanations for dreams, but regardless of these, it is important to know that dreaming is not an indication of a good quality of sleep. Also, having recurrent dreams is a very common experience and not necessarily indicative of any psychological problems.

Ten ways of Improving Sleep

1 Often a good investment towards better sleep is the purchase of new pillows. Likewise, it is important to be comfortable in the bed itself. Be warm with a good duvet or sheets with extra blankets if required. Try to cut down on external noise.

2 Avoid cat naps during the day. Any sleep that you have will detract from night-time sleep and reduce the strength of the bed as the sole stimulus for sleep.

3 Take regular physical exercise and get plenty of fresh air, but not last thing at night.

4 Avoid all stimulant drugs at least two hours prior to going to bed. This includes coffee, tea, Cola drinks, all of which contain caffeine. Switch to milky bedtime drinks such as cocoa. Also avoid smoking prior to going to bed. Do not take slimming pills. Do not use alcohol as a means of getting to sleep, this will simply lead to alcohol dependence and there is evidence that alcohol has a detrimental affect on the quality of your sleep.

5 Try to keep regular hours, getting up at the same time however tired you may feel. Don't be tempted to lie in and snooze if you've had a bad night. Get up and you will more likely sleep better the next night. Try to go to bed only when you're tired but do not stay up past a certain critical time, say one hour after you would normally go to bed.

6 Eliminate most other unecessary activities in bed apart from sleep – do not eat in bed, watch television, or read. These reduce the impression of bed as the place to sleep in your mind and can therefore effect its potency as a stimulus for sleep.

7 Do not eat anything at least two hours before going to bed. The body's digestive processes are less efficient when a person is lying down and indigestion may result.

8 Make sure that your pre-bedtime behaviours are as relaxing as possible. A hot bath, relaxation exercises, or a non-taxing read can all help. Don't go to bed immediately after a period of intense concentration, e.g. working late, playing cards, or following a difficult knitting pattern. The mind may still be active and alert.

139

9 Don't lie awake for ages wondering why you are not sleeping. It is much better to get out of bed and return after a short period when you feel more tired. This breaks the vicious circle of worry, increasing physiological arousal, leading to further worrying, and so on.

10 Perhaps most importantly, try and determine yourself why it is that you're not sleeping. Sometimes we may be able to identify a particular stress or problem which may be affecting us in our inability to sleep. Take active steps towards eliminating or reducing this stress. Your body will soon tell you if you were correct in your hypothesis and effective in your solutions.

Chapter Seven

RUNNING AN ANXIETY MANAGEMENT GROUP

INTRODUCTION

The material presented so far in this book offers an educational, self-help approach to clients' anxiety problems. Such material can be delivered on an individual basis or in a group format. Working in groups offers an enjoyable contrast to individual work and is also an effective form of therapeutic intervention, as well as being a cost-efficient use of time. This chapter will attempt to convey some of our experiences, as well as describing a structured group programme.

CHARACTERISTICS OF ANXIETY MANAGEMENT GROUPS

There is no one way of running these groups or courses, and neither is there a fixed, inflexible agenda. The way a group is run will be heavily influenced by the personal characteristics and style of the therapists involved. However, from our practice certain common characteristics have emerged.

The groups or courses are closed and time limited, usually running initially for either six or eight weeks. Later booster and long term follow-up sessions are arranged for one month, then three months, after completion of the structured programme.

Each session lasts approximately one hour and twenty minutes, and occurs initially on a weekly basis at the same time and place. The final two sessions may be planned at fortnightly intervals to help the group 'tail off'.

Each group or course consists ideally of six or seven clients, all group members having been individually assessed by one of the therapists, using the structured interview and questionnaires described in chapter 3.

The group sits in a circle in a reasonably large room.

The course is based on a psycho-educational model so clients are encouraged to adopt the role of 'active learners' rather than 'passive patients'.

The course is based on the principles of self-help, hence clients are reminded that they have responsibility for their own problems and for changing their own behaviour. Dependency on the therapist is discouraged.

The therapists take on the role of director, facilitator, organizer, reinforcer, and teacher. A co-therapist can make the experience of running the group more enjoyable by taking some of the responsibility off the therapist's shoulders, and reinforcing and consolidating the information. It is also a useful way of transmitting skills to other mental health professionals. If the co-therapist is experienced each can alternate between running different sections of the programme.

Members receive a large amount of information in the form of printed handouts. We prefer to distribute these on a sessional basis, rather than all together in a book form which is given out in the first session, as individual handouts seem to focus attention on the specific issue under discussion.

FOUR MAIN THERAPEUTIC COMPONENTS

Each session contains a mixture of four basic therapeutic ingredients.

Providing Information and Education About Anxiety and Stress

Information in the form of printed handouts and tapes is given out, during all sessions. This helps clients learn to understand more about the processes involved in, for example, stress, or having a panic attack, or the development and maintenance of phobic anxiety, or the uses and abuses of tranquillizers. There appear to be two main benefits from providing clients with information. First, the more they understand 'what is going on', the easier it becomes to do something about it. Very often the clients are unaware of their role in doing things which make their anxiety worse (e.g. hyperventilating, catastrophizing, avoiding, etc.). Once the processes involved have been understood, and a future plan delineated, clients can begin to make positive changes. Second, when people do not know what is happening to them, they become frightened, feel out of control, and are more prone to catastrophic misinterpretations. Simply knowing what is 'going on' reduces anxiety.

Teaching Coping Skills

Clients learn specific skills and techniques for controlling anxiety and reducing stress. These include specific skills for coping with acute, situational anxiety, such as muscle relaxation, programmed physical exercise, respiratory control, distraction techniques, and other cognitive therapy methods. Skills aimed at reducing general levels of stress, such as assertiveness skills, goal planning, and time management are also included in the package. All these particular strategies or skills have the common goal of helping clients feel more in control of both their symptoms of stress, and their life in general. These adaptive coping skills are differentiated from maladaptive coping skills, such as the long-term use of tranquillizers, abusing alcohol, food and drugs, avoiding situations, and behaving in a passive, non-assertive manner.

Setting and Achieving Specific Behavioural Homework Assignments

Expectations are set at an early stage: that the therapist can only offer education and advice, and the client is responsible for assimilating and applying this information. In addition to the practice of self-help skills, all clients, in negotiation with the therapist, will set themselves specific homework tasks to be achieved before the next session. Clients will announce their intentions to the group, and then report back the following week. For individuals with phobic anxiety, these tasks include graded exposure to progressively more difficult avoided situations. For non-phobic clients, homework tasks might include being more assertive in a specific situation at work, involvement in a relaxing leisure activity, or cutting down on prescribed tranquillizers. As well as these individual homework tasks, all

143

clients, whether phobic or non-phobic, carry out the relaxation exercises, and go through a period of self-monitoring of their levels of anxiety.

Meeting and Sharing With Other People With Similar Problems

Clients often feel that they are 'the only one in the world' with this particular complaint. By meeting others 'in the same boat', they begin to feel less alone and different. This can be helpful and reassuring in reducing anxiety. The group also offers clients the opportunity to share experiences and receive feedback from peers. Membership of a group also offers an added social support system. Members often meet up to carry out homework tasks together, and contact each other between sessions. At the end of each course, members are invited to exchange telephone numbers and addresses, and small self-help groups often develop.

AN ANXIETY MANAGEMENT GROUP PROGRAMME

The following structured programme has been designed, modified and run by the authors on numerous occasions over the last five years. We originally started with a six-session package but later increased its length to eight sessions. The handouts referred to on the agenda are based on information discussed in chapters 4, 5, and 6 of this book.

Session 1 – Therapist outlines plan for course and first session – self-help model, components of course emphasized – 3-system model of anxiety – explanation of a model of stress – Tap and Glass metaphor.
  – Introductory name-disclosing game. Members then introduce themselves and briefly outline their problems.
  – Joint reading and discussion of 'Coping with Anxiety' handout (emphasis on introductory model, physical symptoms, benefits of relaxation).
  – Introduce relaxation training – therapist teaches exercises and conducts relaxation practice.
  – Homework – self monitoring/diary sheets – rate anxiety on 0–100 scale – relaxation tapes handed out.

Session 2 – Review homework – individuals give an example from their diary sheets and report on relaxation exercises.

- Joint reading and discussion of manual 'Understanding and Coping with Anxiety' (introduces 3-system model of anxiety, anxiety is normal – physical symptoms).
- Joint reading and discussion of handout 'Acute Hyperventilation'.
- Demonstrate provocation test where clients deliberately over-breath – discuss catastrophic misinterpretation of symptoms – breathing exercises.
- Homework – self-monitoring – relaxation – attempt to carry out disclosed behavioural target.

Session 3 – Review homework – individuals report on targets.

- Joint reading and discussion of manual 'Understanding and Coping with Anxiety' (topics covered include – what maintains anxiety? the role of avoidance behaviour and catastrophic thoughts, panic spirals).
- Look at handout on identifying 'self statements'.
- Individuals start to work out hierarchy of specific behaviours or situations for planned practice.
- Homework – complete hierarchy – attempt to carry out disclosed behavioural target.

Session 4 – Review – individual's targets and completed hierarchy sheets.

- Joint reading and discussion of handout – 'Cognitive Techniques' – 'Distraction' and 'Positive Self-Talk'.
- Joint reading and discussion of handouts 'Positive Self-Statements for Coping with Anxiety'.
- Homework attempt to carry out disclosed behavioural target – workout 'Individual Self Statement Card'.

Session 5 – Review homework tasks.

- Read and discuss handout on 'Thinking Errors – Looking for Rational Answers'.
- Read and discuss handout 'Irrational Beliefs' – individuals identify personal and most relevant belief.

145

    – Read and discuss 'Stress Control' handout.
    – Homework – attempt to carry out disclosed behavioural target.
Session 6 – Review homework tasks.
    – Read and discuss handout on 'Assertiveness' – differentiating between communication styles – assertive, passive, aggressive.
    – Individuals identify specific situations where they are not assertive.
    – Homework – attempt disclosed assertiveness task.
Session 7 – Review homework tasks.
    – Read and discuss handout 'Goal Planning'.
    – Individuals decide on own goals, objectives, achievements.
    – Homework – attempt specific behaviour task.
Session 8 – Review homework tasks.
    – Read and discuss 'Common Questions about Anxiety' – topics include – dealing with setbacks, uses of tranquillizers, keeping practice going, are you getting enough fun out of life?
    – Exchange telephone numbers – possibilities for self-help systems.
    – Homework – target to achieve by five-week follow-up group.

EXPERIENCES AND ADVICE ON RUNNING GROUPS

The following section contains some experiences and advice on how to run an anxiety management group.

The first session is the most important because if it is not run properly it also may be the last session for some clients. The most noticeable feature of this session is that everybody is very anxious. The therapist has to work hard to reduce the general level of anxiety and they should present as being relaxed, confident, and reassuring. It is worth pointing out to the group that the first session is always the most anxiety-provoking, after which future sessions become progressively easier. Make this point firmly, because the idea of anxiety-reduction with repeated exposure is one of the fundamental principles of the course. Try to introduce some humour into the session, as there is no better way of reducing anxiety than to have the group laughing together. Offer an escape route, by pointing out the whereabouts of the toilet, if you notice a particular member is looking exceptionally bad.

We have found it useful to ask all group members to read, in turn, and aloud, sections of the printed handouts that have been distributed before they are discussed. This is usually an anxiety-provoking experience and some members might try to avoid doing it. It is important at this stage to stress the unhealthy nature of avoidance. Explain that the whole purpose of the course is to learn how to control anxiety symptoms. Reading a paragraph in front of others offers a great opportunity to both provoke and control anxiety. Redefine the problem in terms of a challenge, ask them to take two steps backwards and treat it as an experiment. Emphasize that it does not matter how badly one reads the paragraph as long as the situation is not avoided. Make a joke of 'who is the worst reader'. In one group it happened that every week the same woman would say, 'I can't read that, it makes me too nervous. My eyes go all funny, I can't concentrate'. We would always suggest firmly that she read her paragraph and reluctantly she would do so. She was a warm, good-natured person with a sense of humour. In the sixth session, on Assertiveness Training, she insisted in a very assertive tone that she was not reading her paragraph. The whole group burst out laughing and agreed that on that occasion she should be 'let off' her reading.

It is important to avoid using jargon and complicated language. The principles of the course must be made to seem very simple, and are best explained in everyday language and metaphor (see chapter 4).

At the beginning of each session review homework assignments. Go around the group and have everybody in turn explain a particular example of their coping, or the task they set themselves during the preceding week. Try to emphasize the positive; praise and reinforce achievements. Use people's experiences to support the cognitive–behavioural model. Encourage members to talk about their experiences in terms of the cognitive–behavioural three-system model. A series of positive reports regarding homework tasks can set the tone of the group to follow. The 'domino effect' is often very noticeable; one person's comments, whether positive or negative, influence the person who follows. It is sometimes a good idea to start homework reporting with a client who you recognize as a likely positive contributor.

Towards the end of each session when clients are setting themselves homework tasks, make a point of writing down on a piece of paper, in specific terms, what it is they are supposed to do. Do not accept woolly generalizations, such as 'Oh, I'll try to do something next week' or 'I think, I'm going to a party'. The homework assignment must be specific and concrete, requiring the deliberate confrontation of anxiety; this does not mean doing something that they are already going to do anyway. The homework assignment involves setting a task that they would not normally do.

Some clients might put forward the excuse that there is really nothing that they avoid and so they cannot set themselves any homework tasks. Don't accept this for one minute. Everybody has situations that they are inclined to avoid because they provoke some anxiety. Individuals with phobic anxiety are relatively easy; catching buses, going in lifts, and standing in queues are good examples of tasks. The individual with generalized anxiety might set him/herself the task of reviving an old leisure activity such as horse-riding or swimming, or inviting a neighbour around for coffee. The perfectionist who announces 'I avoid nothing because of anxiety' is again fooling him/herself as they strive to do everything perfectly all the time, because not to do so creates anxiety. So, the perfectionist might be instructed to do something wrong at work, or deliberately blemish their appearance, or turn up to the group five minutes late. All these situations create anxiety which the client then has to cope with.

One illuminating example of the usefulness of behavioural homework targets is that provided by a lift-phobic whom we saw. A phobia of lifts often arises within the more complex agoraphobic syndrome and, with the right approach, is not too difficult to break. Like any phobia, the lift phobia is maintained by avoidance and a network of catastrophic thoughts. Encourage clients to identify their own personal chain of catastrophic thoughts. In one recent group one woman had not been in a lift for twenty years. With prompting, her chain of catastrophic thoughts were identified: 'The lift will get stuck'. 'They will not be able to get me out'. 'I'll be in there for days'. 'I won't have any food or water'. 'I'll starve'. This bizarre image at the bottom of this chain of catastrophic thoughts has a little old lady, starving and thirsty, a human skeleton, huddled in the corner of a glass-fronted lift in a busy department store. When this network of catastrophic thoughts and fantasies was exposed, it seemed bizarre and ridiculous. The therapist and the group jointly answered those irrational statements, and everyone could see the funny side of the bizarre nature of her final image. That lady successfully went into a glass-fronted lift the next week armed with instructions on relaxation, deep breathing, and an index card with positive self-statements in her pocket. Her evident pleasure and pride in her achievement spilled over into the group, motivating others to follow suit and try out situations they had been avoiding. This one simple example had shown the woman in question, and the group, that people could change and did not have to be slaves to their anxiety.

Another good homework task for some clients is to encourage them to go and try deliberately to provoke and control a panic attack. Their recently acquired understanding very often prevents them from achieving a full-blown panic attack. It seems that once people fully understand what a panic attack is, they are no longer frightened of the physical symptoms, and no longer have catastrophic thoughts: they find it almost impossible to have a full-blown panic attack. The role of a positive mental set, i.e. deliberately looking out for a panic attack as an opportunity to practice self-control techniques, rather than running away from it, supports the school of thought that views a panic attack as largely cognitive–behavioural in nature.

Individuals will take on different roles within the group. It is useful for the therapist to be aware of who their allies are, those who can act as a positive role model, and which members are going to be resistant. The positive role models should be encouraged to help other group members by explaining ideas and concepts, and offering encouragement and confrontation. The notion of asking 'circular questions' is a helpful way of developing these interactions, i.e. 'Mrs Smith, you had a similar experience to Mr White, how did you cope?', or 'You've taken tranquillizers in the past and gave them up, what would you say to somebody like Mrs Jones?'

ADVANTAGES AND DISADVANTAGES OF GROUP TREATMENTS

Advantages of Group Treatment

Cost effectiveness For an eight-session course, with eight members, clients receive approximately twelve hours of therapist contact time. This is at the comparatively small cost of three hours therapy time per individual if there are two therapists running a group (one and a half hours of therapy time per individual if there is one therapist).

Opportunities for sharing and reducing feelings of loneliness Clients often report that they stop seeing themselves as abnormal when they meet others in a similar situation. The group also offers support for individuals going through difficult periods.

'Positive modelling' and peer reinforcement If a client has successfully carried out a difficult homework task the group can reinforce this success more powerfully than a therapist alone. Similarly, positive achievements act as good models and encourage other members into action.

Opportunities for feedback The group is an ideal setting for clients to test out assumptions they might have about themselves. Feedback from peers can be a powerful mirror, showing clients how things are, rather than how they assume they are.

Opportunities for continuing support The group can easily become a network of support during and after the course. Self-help groups can develop out of such structured programmes.

A structured group This offers a time limited contract and very definite expectations of therapist intervention. These limits help to focus clients' motivation and endeavours towards self-help in the independent management of their problems.

Disadvantages of Group Treatment

Reduced time for the idiosyncrasies of clients' problems Because of time restriction it is impossible to be excessively responsive to

150

individual needs. Individuals with more complicated problems, that do not easily fit into the overall structure of the programme, may either be neglected or take up an inappropriate amount of group time. This serves to emphasize the importance of a good early assessment to decide on the client's suitability for group treatment.

Effort of setting up a group It is obviously easier to make an appointment with an individual than organize a group, although once a format programme has been decided, handouts printed, and a venue organized, most of the other organizational tasks can be carried out by clerical and secretarial staff. Potential group members are interviewed, then placed on the waiting list for the next group, and contacted when the group starts.

SELECTION OF GROUP MEMBERS

All clients are individually assessed by the therapist running the group, before the course starts. The semi-structured interview and the questionnaires described in chapter 3 are the main forms of assessment. Further questionnaires are then completed at the end of the eight-week programme and at three months follow-up.

In our selection procedure we are looking for three main characteristics. First, the problem presented by the client must be of the type that will be responsive to the structured group programme. Clients with panic attacks, phobic anxiety, and generalized anxiety appear particularly suitable, because the programme has been designed to meet their needs. Clients where anxiety is secondary to another major problem, e.g. a formal mental illness, clinical depression, major marital dysfunction, or an eating disorder are not suitable and, in our experience, do not do particularly well in this type of group. Second, clients need to be reasonably well motivated to make changes themselves, and to accept the basic self-help principles of the group. It helps if in the assessment interview, the client can delineate specific objectives and targets to achieve; this gives some indicator of clients' motivation and a target to aim for. Third, clients may need to be prepared to wait until the start of the next course, which might not be for up to two months. For

individuals with phobic anxiety and longstanding anxiety problems, this is often not a problem, however for those in a state of
crisis, immediate individual sessions may be more appropriate.
Indeed, this type of group is not particularly suitable for those
individuals in such a crisis, as they may not be able to concentrate on the material presented. Our experience indicates that
the majority of in-patients in psychiatric hospitals are not
particularly suitable, even if their major problem is anxiety.
Admission to a psychiatric hospital usually suggests anxiety
levels above the level needed to absorb the material in the group,
a state of immediate crisis, and usually significant prescribing of
anxiolytic medication.

The make-up of any one particular group merits some consideration. In our experience mixed groups, for example,
stressed business executives sitting alongside agoraphobic
housewives, can work well, as long as there is at least one other
person in the group with similar problems. A group of seven
female phobics with only one male with generalized anxiety or
vice-versa can be problematic.

FINDINGS FROM RESEARCH

Anxiety management treatment packages delivered through a
group format rather than individually have been described by
Eayrs *et al.* (1984), Jupp and Dudley (1984), Johnson (1975), and
Powell (1987). All four studies have demonstrated the effectiveness of these types of programmes and found that anxiety levels
fell significantly. When group treatment packages are compared
with individual treatments the results are very similar, using
similar psychometric assessments as outcome measures.

In the research carried out by one of the present authors
(Powell 1987), forty seven clients in six separate structured
group programmes were asked to rate which components of the
package they had found most helpful. Clients rated receiving
'information about anxiety and stress', and 'Being in the group
and meeting others with similar problems' as the most helpful
parts of the treatment package. These two aspects of treatment
were rated significantly higher than any of the other components such as homework tasks, or learning coping skills such as
relaxation or positive self-talk. This result would seem to have

implications for clinical practice. Perhaps it is time we placed less emphasis on our role as individual therapists teaching specialist skills, and moved towards the position of educators and organizers of self-help services.

A further interesting result was that individuals' perception of the causes of their anxiety shifted significantly away from the belief that there was something physically wrong with them. As we had hoped, clients' catastrophic thoughts, particularly mis-interpretations of bodily symptoms, altered significantly. Similarly, use of maladaptive coping strategies such as avoidance behaviour, taking tranquillizers, and visiting their GP, decreased, while the adoption of adaptive coping strategies, such as relaxation, increased.

A further unpublished project attempted to assess the anxiety characteristics of the type of client who benefited most from the treatment package. During the initial assessment interview clients were rated by the interviewer on a number of four-point scales. These scales included such characteristics as frequency of panic attacks, generalized anxiety, avoidance behaviour, psychiatric history, worry about anxiety, interest in the approach, use of anxiolytic medication, and recent life stresses. Two scales showed a correlation with positive changes on an outcome measure – Spielberger State Anxiety Inventory. These two scales were 'worry about anxiety' and 'interest in the approach'. This is only a preliminary finding, based on the interviewer's subjective assessment, but could be the basis for future research. The notion that clients could be rated on a dimension of how worried they were about their symptoms of stress (physical, cognitive, behavioural) as opposed to how worried they were about factors which caused those symptoms (Stress's, Life Events, etc.) is an interesting and as yet unexplored area.

Chapter Eight

SOME CASE-STUDY EXAMPLES OF TREATING ANXIETY AND STRESS

INTRODUCTION

This final chapter is an attempt to demonstrate the integration and application of the academic and practical information contained in the preceding chapters. The cases have been chosen to reflect the breadth of clinical problems subsumed under the diagnostic category of anxiety disorders. We have also tried to represent the types of client problems which commonly present in clinical practice. The approach to the assessment, formulation, and treatment of these disorders is cognitive behavioural in nature.

The cases are based upon actual clients treated by the authors in the course of their routine clinical practice. In each case the original referral letter that we received is reproduced in full. The names and specific details have been changed to ensure clients' anonymity.

CASE 1: SIMPLE PHOBIA

Referral Letter From Client's General Practitioner

'This young lady has a phobia of spiders. She came to see me recently in a very distressed state saying this problem was 'ruining her life'. She mentioned seeing a television programme recently when a person with a phobia was given a 'flooding' treatment and she requested similar help. I would be most grateful if you would see her and offer any help that you can. In all other repsects she seems a very competent, sensible and intelligent young lady.'

Presenting Problem

At the initial assessment interview this 26-year-old woman described a lifelong fear of spiders. This fear was apparently under control until approximately six months ago when she moved from central London into a relatively rural and isolated cottage on the Berkshire Downs. She described her new home as infested with spiders and this was incapacitating her to the point of being unable to enter a room for fear it may contain a spider. Matters came to a head one week prior to the initial referral from her general practitioner when Ms Jones swerved her car, crashing into a lamp-post, when she caught sight of a small black spider running across her car dashboard and she panicked.

On encountering a spider Ms Jones would invariably experience severe panic and run away. In the past she had been able to get near enough to small spiders to kill them, but now found herself too terrified to face the spider under any circumstances. Though her fears were primarily related to house spiders she would also feel acutely uncomfortable with larger varieties of garden spider.

Ms Jones had no fear of any other insects including those, such as crane flies and water boatmen, which may be considered spider-like. She had difficulty in identifying the exact nature of the fear but believed it had something to do with a spider's rapid, unpredictable movement and ominous look.

She was under no irrational illusions regarding a spider's potential to harm her physically.

Background

Ms Jones was the youngest of three girls. She described her childhood as very happy, having had many friends, and being bright at school. Ms Jones described her father as rather aloof and lacking in emotion but felt that this deficit was easily compensated for by her mother, who thoroughly spoilt her as a child.

Ms Jones' academic abilities enabled her to read a degree in Biology at university. Though she studied all insects including spiders on her course she did not have any opportunity to work specifically with the latter. Indeed even the theoretical study of

155

spiders became so difficult at one point that she needed considerable persuasion to complete her course.

On completing her degree Ms Jones had worked subsequently as a scientist for a pharmaceutical company. She enjoyed her work and her recent move was for promotion within the company. She had built up a large social network within a short time of moving house and, together with her boyfriend, had an active social life. Ms Jones currently had little contact with her sisters, who both lived abroad, but regularly visited her mother and father. She reported no history of psychological problems in her family, other than in her eldest sister who had a marked phobia of all types of insect as a child whereby she would scream hysterically for hours on seeing such a creature. She appeared however to overcome this during adolescence and now experienced only minor difficulties.

Ms Jones reported that her mother had taken great trouble throughout her childhood to ensure that she and her sister rarely encountered the creatures they feared. Her mother would check rooms thoroughly for spiders at Ms Jones' request and would always come to her assistance if alerted by Ms Jones' screams, quickly despatch the spider then reassure her daughter copiously of her safety. This protective mantle had more recently been taken up by Ms Jones' boyfriend with whom she had lived for the past three years.

Assessment

Extensive questioning at interview failed to highlight any generalization of the fear of spiders to other objects or situations. The 'Fear Inventory' confirmed that Ms Jones exhibited a mono-symptomatic phobia of spiders. The 'Effects of Life Inventory' indicated the problem was most evident in the home and had little effect on other aspects of life. Regarding physical symptoms Ms Jones' questionnaire highlighted feeling faint, nauseous, and having severe palpitations on encountering spiders. She also described at times being totally immoblized by her fear.

Formulation of Problem

Seligman (1971) has suggested that some humans may be biologically prepared or predisposed to fear certain stimuli, that may have actually once been dangerous to our species. Thus snakes, spiders, blood, and heights would more rapidly condition phobic responses than say flowers or leaves. It is possible that in the case of Ms Jones this biological predisposition was very strong and that this fact underlied her current fears.

In addition to any biological factors it seems likely that Ms Jones' response towards spiders may at least in part be learned from her eldest sister. Bandura (1969) has demonstrated that much of what we learn is learned through a process of 'modelling', whereby an individual observes another (the model) engaged in a behaviour that is ignored, punished, or rewarded. Then in a similar situation the observer will imitate the models behaviour. Clearly Ms Jones will have watched or heard her sister exhibiting a fear response to an insect and have been immediately rewarded with the sympathetic attention and concern of her mother. Exhibiting this type of response was equally rewarded for Ms Jones by her mother and subsequently her boyfriend. This reinforcement may have occurred differentially, mostly in the home, which may account for Ms Jones expressing greater fear for house spiders.

Finally, since Ms Jones's mother went to great lengths to ensure her daughter would not encounter spiders in the family home, she was able to successfully avoid the feared stimulus. Avoiding will always make subsequent encounters with things we fear increasingly difficult.

Treatment Procedures

Though it is possible to use the technique of flooding, as mentioned by the general practitioner for fears of this type, in view of Ms Jones extreme anxiety to even small spiders, this method was discounted. Flooding is a technique whereby an individual is required to encounter the feared stimuli at the top of their fear hierarchy in the first treatment session. Extreme anxiety is created, but the client eventually learns to control this and learns that they can survive the experience. Realizing that their catastrophic prophecies of having a heart attack, or dying, or whatever, when confronted by their worst fear were irrational, clients learn very quickly to overcome fear with repeated exposure. Flooding may also be effected in imagination where a worst possible scenario may be played out. This technique is sometimes called implosion. Flooding a spider phobic might involve for example confronting them with a large black house spider let loose on their lap!

The hypothesis for the development of Ms Jones' problem was discussed with her. She reported being very grateful to have her problems explained to her in this way and was reassured that 'somebody understands'. The next stage was to explain the physical, behavioural, and cognitive features of Ms Jones fear response within a model of stress and to reassure her that these were very common in phobias and that gradually she would learn to control these. The overall proposed treatment techniques were then discussed and agreed upon.

Having engaged Ms Jones' boyfriend in treatment and having asked him to co-operate in not helping to make it easy for her to avoid dealing with spiders, the next stage to helping Ms Jones overcome her phobia was to help her to construct her fear hierarchy. Taking different spider characteristics in turn, it was slowly possible to establish that Ms Jones was least fearful of pictures of spiders and most afraid of large black house spiders greater than one and a half inches in diameter. In time we established a total of fourteen different experiences of spiders, increasing in fear.

The next stage was to teach Ms Jones progressive muscular relaxation. This was important for two reasons. First, it gave Ms Jones a sense of personal control over her fear reaction and was used susbequently to reduce her anxiety level each time she encountered and dealt with a spider outside the therapy sessions. Second, at the end of each session progressive muscular relaxation was used to help to reduce any anxiety which may have developed as a result of Ms Jones' encounter with spiders in the therapy session. This latter point is important. Clients must not leave this type of therapy with high levels of anxiety if they are to be expected to return.

Additionally, prior to the active treatment phase a scale of subjective units of distress (SUD) was agreed upon from 1–100, where 1 represents minimal or no anxiety, and 100 represents maximum anxiety. This scale was used in both the drawing up of the fear hierarchy and during the encounters with the feared stimuli.

The specific fear hierarchy constructed was as follows:

14 Handling a large ($1\frac{1}{2}''$) black house spider   100   SUD
13 Recapturing large black house spider in jam
    jar ($1\frac{1}{2}''$)   95
12 Handling live black house spider 1"   90
11 Handling live black house spider $\frac{3}{4}''$ 85
10 Handling live black house spider $\frac{1}{2}''$ 80
 9 Handling large dead black house spider
    ($1\frac{1}{2}''$)   70
 8 Handling small ($\frac{1}{4}''$) live black house spider   60
 7 Handling dead house spider (size $\frac{3}{4}''$)   55 predicted
 6 Handling live garden spider (size $\frac{1}{2}''$)   50   levels
 5 Handling small ($\frac{1}{2}''$) dead black house spider   40
 4 Handling small ($\frac{1}{4}''$) dead black house spider   35
 3 Handling a 'money spider'   30
 2 Looking at photographs of spiders   20
 1 Looking at cartoon and self drawings of
    spiders   15
 1 General discussion about spiders   10   SUD

Each treatment session of one hour aimed to deal with two items from the hierarchy, one being the previous highest from the last session and the other being the next item on the list. As a homework exercise Ms Jones was asked to work with the lower item of the two from the session.

Both dead and live spiders were placed centrally on a white piece of paper in the centre of the desk, live spiders being contained in a jam jar. Therapist and client sat opposite each other. Ms Jones was asked to identify her SUD level at this point and at intervals thereafter until the level dropped sufficiently and she had the confidence to proceed. Ms Jones was then asked to try to touch the dead spider with a pen and gradually to substitute the pen for her finger. As the initial anxiety reduced she attempted to pick up the spider and place it on her hand. With the dead spiders she was eventually required to pass the spider from hand to hand so as to simulate vitality in the spider. The therapist offered verbal praise and encouragement throughout the session.

Gradually Ms Jones was able to proceed through her fear hierarchy smoothly, to her great delight and the delight of her boyfriend, without any of the intense fear reactions she had predicted. In the fourth week of treatment she found a small black spider in the bath at home and dispatched it without help from her boyfriend. In the weeks of her sixth and seventh sessions she deliberately set out to find spiders in her home and dealt with those she found, initially killing them and eventually learning to trap them in a jam jar and throw them outside.

After a total of eight one-hour sessions Ms Jones was confidently handling large black house spiders. Although at a one-year follow-up she still reported a mild initial surge of anxiety on encountering large house spiders she had dealt with numerous such encounters without major difficulty.

CASE 2: STRESS, TYPE-A BEHAVIOUR, AND AGGRESSION

Referral Letter from Client's General Practitioner

'I would be grateful if you could see this stressed 35-year-old man, who came to see me today in a very agitated state, saying he was extremely worried about his aggression. He feels he is on the verge of "doing something really stupid". His recent aggressive outbursts have adversely affected his marriage, and his wife is talking about a permanent separation and divorce, however, he is very keen for his family to stay together. I think he is also having difficulties at work. I do not know him very well, as he rarely comes to the surgery, but he seems a very down to earth, competent, genuine man, looking for some professional help.'

Presenting Problems

Mr Bird presented as a likeable, friendly, well-built man in his mid-thirties, who initially found the assessment interview quite difficult. He said, 'I never thought it would come to this ... visiting a shrink.' As the interview progressed he noticeably relaxed and seemed relieved to be able to tell his story. He reported his main problems as follows.

Over the last six months he had become increasingly irritable and aggressive with his colleagues at work, and more importantly with his wife and two children. In a recent outburst at work he pinned a colleague to the wall, was verbally abusive, and out of control. He later tended his resignation but was talked out of it by other colleagues. He was also involved in an incident at a local dance when he again became very threatening. So far he had not hit anybody, but he said that he felt 'wound up like a coiled spring' most of the time.

His marital relationship over the last few months had become very strained. He and his wife had arguments followed by black moods where neither would speak to each other for days. Recently Mr Bird left home for ten days and went to stay with his mother. This move was suggested by his wife who insisted that she could no longer stand his aggression and bad moods. Mr Bird desperately wanted his marriage to work reporting that, 'my wife and kids are my whole life, but I'm just driving them away.' He felt that he was solely to blame for the marital problems, saying, 'it's not a case for marriage guidance, it's me, there is something wrong with me'.

Mr Bird reported getting severe headaches recently and feeling very tense in his neck and shoulder. His doctor had also informed him that he had high blood pressure, and this had made Mr Bird worry about having a heart attack.

He reported generally feeling tense and miserable, dissatisfied with himself and his life in general.

Background

Mr Bird had worked as a charge-hand and machine-setter in the same engineering company for the last thirteen years. He married Doreen fourteen years ago, and described their relationship as 'turbulent'. They had separated on two occasions: recently, when Mr Bird went to stay with his mother for ten days, and twelve years ago when his wife became depressed just after the birth of their first child. He described their sex life as 'infrequent'. They have two children, aged twelve and aged eight, whom he described as 'overpowering bundles of fun'. The family also kept a number of pets including dogs, ducks, and geese.

Mr Bird was the oldest of five children, having three younger brothers and one sister. His father was a factory worker, and was described as being 'quick–tempered and aggressive'. He played football and gambled, always giving a hundred per cent and he encouraged his sons to develop the same competitive aggressive streak. He described his mother as 'magic, a great smoother over of situations'. Mr Bird described one of his younger brothers and his younger sister as being even more aggressive than himself. He felt close to all members of his family, although his wife did not get on with his father and one of his younger brothers. Mr Bird described his childhood as uneventful. He was always good at sports at school but not very good academically. He remembered always being in fights at school but nothing particularly serious.

Mr Bird acknowledged that he had always been a rather aggressive character, enjoying all competitive sports, especially football, cricket, and squash. He felt that, like his father, he had 'the killer instinct'. His wife had never liked his aggressive characteristics and he reported that they nearly broke up on their wedding day because Mr Bird got very angry with some of his friends for 'messing up' the car that was taking them on their honeymoon.

Mr Bird no longer played football but for the last three years had coached a boys 'under tens' football team. Recently one of the other fathers had become involved and had taken over most of the managerial responsibilities of the team. He felt dissatisfied with his new role and now felt that he was no more than a 'bag boy'. Only three weeks ago Mr Bird embarrassed himself at a match when he started shouting and bawling at one of the boys for not pulling his weight. Some of the other parents thought that his behaviour was inappropriate.

At work a major recent source of stress had been that he felt that he had been passed over for promotion because of his irascibility. Unfortunately, the person who was promoted above him was an old enemy and somebody Mr Bird completely despised. He said he had no respect for him because he was 'a child who didn't know how to handle men'. The recent incident at work where Mr Bird became very aggressive and resigned (although he later withdrew his resignation) was a result of this newly promoted rival giving Mr Bird a written warning for lack of punctuality. He said he felt very wound up at work now and often snapped at the smallest provocation. He had a number of friends but had not had much contact with them recently. Although he was close to his brothers he found it difficult to talk to them about personal matters.

Assessment

Mr Bird completed our battery of brief screening questionnaires before the first assessment interview. On the 'Hospital Anxiety and Depression Questionnaire' both scores for anxiety and depression suggested clinically significant problems. On the 'Physical Symptoms Inventory' symptoms such as muscle tension, headaches, and hot flushes were most pronounced. On the 'Cognitive Anxiety Questionnaire' the two thoughts that occurred quite often were 'I'm going to have a heart attack', 'I'm going to go mad', and a further anxiety provoking thought was 'my aggression is driving my loved ones away from me'. Mr Bird scored less than five on the 'Fear Inventory', demonstrating no noticeable phobic avoidance tendencies. On the 'Effects on Life Inventory', high scores appeared on the scales of work, social leisure activities, family life, and intimate relationships. In a later session Mr Bird completed the Type-A Behaviour Questionnaire and scored very highly.

Formulation of Problem

Mr Bird came across in the assessment interview as a man under stress. His difficulties exemplify how primary stresses, produce worrying symptoms – in his case aggression, headaches, and high blood pressure – which in themselves become secondary stresses: an upwardly spiralling vicious circle of anxiety leading to anxiety soon became established.

Mr Bird's premorbid personality certainly seemed one which might have made him particularly vulnerable to certain stresses. He admitted he had always been 'a hard driving competitive person with a short fuse and a tendency to fly off the handle'. Obviously his father and brothers with similar predispositions acted as important role models and as reinforcers of that style. It seemed likely that Mr Bird's Type A behaviour had for most of his life been channelled into sporting activities. An outlet he no longer pursued.

Mr Bird had been under a number of stresses recently. The most noticeable being at work where he had been passed over for promotion. Disappointment and frustration were exacerbated by the appointment of a colleague whom he 'despised'. Going to work had become a considerable stress and he admitted that he felt very tense for the first couple of hours each day. Alongside this Mr Bird had been less physically active over the last two years after retiring from playing regular football. His energies had been displaced into coaching a boys' football team, an experience he had recently found demanding, frustrating, and stressful. These background stresses seemed to have increased Mr Bird's predisposition to become irritable and verbally aggressive. A number of incidents where he became aggressive at work, at home, and in leisure had given him cause to worry as had the physical symptoms of headaches and high blood pressure. At home Mr Bird found it difficult to relax as his young children were very demanding. However, the most worrying and stressful aspect of the situation for Mr Bird had been his wife's reaction which had been to cast doubts on the continuation of their marriage. The brief separation increased Mr Bird's awareness of how important his family was to him and now his primary worry was that his marriage would fail. Mr Bird has lost contact with a number of old friends and felt that he had nobody he could talk to properly about the situation. He recognized that he was caught up in something which he didn't fully understand and he was unsure what to do for the best.

Treatment

The first stage of treatment started in the assessment interview allowing Mr Bird to express himself, and ventilate his feelings something he was not used to doing. The next stage involved feeding back to Mr Bird an interpretation and means of understanding what was happening – demystifying the situation – allowing him to identify the primary stresses, the symptoms or results of stress, the secondary stresses, and the resulting vicious circle that he was caught up in. Mr Bird said that he felt wonderfully relieved having talked about it 'man to man', and having gained a clearer understanding of what exactly was going on.

The next stage involved breaking this vicious circle. At the end of the assessment interview he started self-monitoring, recording episodes of increased tension and aggression, and identifying the external and internal triggers and his responses in terms of his thoughts, physical feelings, and behaviour. He also recorded how he coped with these situations. He found the exercise useful saying that it helped him, 'to take a couple of steps back', and look more objectively at how he was behaving. In the second session he was introduced to relaxation training and subsequently given a relaxation tape and told to practise daily at home. He reported that he found these methods particularly useful for reducing his general level of arousal and more specifically for relieving his headaches. He also reported that he used other strategies such as having a warm shower to relax himself when he started feeling tense.

Later we looked at styles of communicating, comparing and differentiating between passive, assertive, and aggressive styles. He found the models understandable and interesting, readily identifying his own predominantly aggressive style. A number of situations were identified as homework assignments in which he felt he could try to be more assertive and less aggressive. One of these situations involved speaking directly and honestly to his manager at work about how difficult he was finding the appointment of his old rival whom he did not like. Another situation involved informing a work colleague in a calm, assertive manner that he did not want him borrowing his tools anymore. A further situation involved talking to his wife about how he felt without raising his voice. The idea that each situation or interaction had a particular aim or goal, namely to get his message across without being aggressive, appealed to Mr Bird's competitive nature.

Mr Bird also began to make decisions about reducing the stresses he was under by rearranging his life. He stopped coaching the 'under tens' football team; he got rid of a number of pet animals which he found he was continually looking after. He also started going swimming with his children one evening a week, and fishing with his son at weekends. He began making an effort to do things together with his wife, such as going out for meals. They also agreed that every evening they would deliberately make a point of sitting down together over a meal and talking about their respective days, rather than either eating in front of the television, or eating separately.

Mr Bird was seen for only five sessions over a period of three months, with one follow-up session three months later. At the end of three months on all the assessment questionnaires his scores had dropped significantly, he had not had a serious aggressive outburst for months, his marriage had improved, and he no longer had headaches. He was appreciative of the time spent by the therapist and felt that it had helped him enormously.

CASE 3: AGORAPHOBIA WITH PANIC ATTACKS

Referral Letter From Community Psychiatric Nurse

'Thank you for seeing this 34-year-old patient who has a long history of anxiety symptoms which she says she would like very much to learn to control for herself. She had been attending a medical hypnotist privately and had found his techniques useful but difficult to do when she is under stress. She has also been seen by two psychiatrists some time ago and has in the past taken diazepam and propranolol. Her only medication currently is 1 milligram of lorazepam daily.'

Presenting Problem

Mrs Evans cancelled the initial appointment that she was offered, explaining that she had felt a litle better recently. However, approximately one month later she rang the department again requesting help.

At her initial presentation she explained the problem was basically one of 'trying to cope with life'. When asked to be more specific she explained that throughout her life she had lacked confidence and always felt inferior. From the age of 17, without remission, she had been experiencing regular panic attacks, occurring in various situations but often if she was required to go shopping or otherwise leave her home. She had not been able to use public transport for approximately ten years and had no friends or social life outside her immediate family. Mrs Evans had been married to her present husband for sixteen years, he being her first boyfriend. The couple decided from the outset that they did not want to have children. Though she felt the marriage was generally good she felt unable to confide her problems in her husband since she believed he would not understand.

Mrs Evans vividly described her first panic attack some seventeen years ago. She was shopping in a crowded supermarket and suddenly became very hot and disorientated. She reported suddenly wanting to take off all her clothes as she felt stifled and unable to breathe, as though choking. She ran out of the shop and straight home, going immediately to bed.

Her mother called out their GP, who diagnosed anxiety.

Subsequently Mrs Evans had remained terrified that she would faint, be sick or otherwise make an exhibition of herself in public. Her symptoms of panic included palpitations, breathlessness, feeling dizzy and faint, feeling nauseous, and sweating. At such times she also had a feeling of unreality as though looking out at the world from inside a thin capsule. As a result of her difficulties Mr Evans had done the couple's shopping for many years. Mrs Evans had approximately three panic attacks per week but recognized she would have daily attacks if her life was not so restricted.

Mrs Evans stated she was very anxious about seeing someone new concerning her difficulties which was why she had postponed the first appointment. However, after two recent severe panic attacks she felt once more that she desperately needed help.

Background Details

Mrs Evans had happy recollections of her childhood in Birmingham. She described her father as a very quiet and shy man who spent much of his time on his allotment. Her mother was also quiet but more timid than her father. Apparently Mrs Evans' mother was the victim of an attacker when she was in her early twenties. The details of this incident were very patchy and were something of a family secret, a taboo subject for her parents. Mrs Evans knew that something had caused her mother to be very wary of the outside world and to impose an anxious watch upon her daughter at all times.

Mrs Evans has one sister, two years older than herself. Her sister was something of a rebel and she recalled on many occasions how her mother's curfews were frequently ignored by her sister. When she was still very young Mrs Evans felt that her parents had rather given up trying to discipline her sister and redoubled their efforts with their second daughter.

Mrs Evans recalled being bullied as a child in her early years at junior school, being physically small and rather timid. However, she eventually made friends with some older girls who agreed to protect her in return for money and sweets. This arrangement went on for many years, until she eventually left school at the age of sixteen. Although she was bright by her teachers' assessment she felt unable to do any public exams, feeling frightened and becoming very upset at the prospect, so she left school with no paper qualifications.

On leaving school she worked part time on the production line in a local factory. It was there that she met and married her husband who worked as the site foreman. Soon afterwards the couple moved to Reading as her husband was offered a better job. They had lived in Reading for fifteen years and though they were generally happy Mrs Evans worried for the health of her parents, though neither of them had been ill in any way.

Mrs Evans had worked for spells, part-time mostly, in cleaning work since their move, lacking the confidence to seek full-time employment. Her husband had always driven her to and from work each evening. She spent much of the rest of her time in a severe ritual of cleaning her house from top to bottom on a daily basis. This routine had become her rationale for not going out, 'I simply haven't got the time'.

Mrs Evans was very vague about her meeting with the two psychiatrists both of whom she saw in the space of six months, three to four years ago. One of these psychiatrists offered her the chance to attend daily at a therapeutic community, but she felt unable to comply with this advice, making various excuses relating to travelling, financial implications, and her fear of strangers. Mrs Evans did take up the offer of medication and reported initially experiencing marked benefit from diazepam and propranolol though these effects did not last. Currently she was taking occasional lorazepam tablets prescribed by her general practitioner. She reported being reluctant, however, to take medication in the long term.

Assessment Procedures

In addition to two hour-long assessment interviews, Mrs Evans was asked to complete a battery of rating scales and questionnaires. These included the Gambrill-Richey assertiveness questionnaire (1975), the 'Hospital Anxiety and Depression Scale', the 'Physical Symptoms Inventory', the 'Cognitive Anxiety Questionnaire', the 'Fear Inventory', and the 'Effects on Life Inventory'.

Mrs Evans responses confirmed the impression gained at interview that she was chronically lacking in self-confidence and assertiveness skills. She scored highly on the questionnaires for anxiety and moderately on the depression scale. She admitted a number of fears not mentioned at interview and found her problems severely effected her lifestyle in all areas sampled by the questionnaire.

Formulation

The pattern of development of Mrs Evans' problems was a fairly typical one. Life-long lack of self-confidence and a general fear of people led to her first panic attack at the age of seventeen. Immediate and subsequent avoidance of the fear situation reduced the likelihood of subsequent panic attacks and was thus reinforced. Friends and family conspired to allow avoidance by 'helping out' doing the feared tasks and Mrs Evans circle of safety for going out gradually reduced.

It seems likely that Mrs Evans had inherited some of her trait anxiety from parents who themselves were shy and retiring. Additionally her 'family secret' made Mrs Evans wary of the outside world and her fears were reinforced by her mother's overprotectiveness and her experiences of being bullied and paying extortion money at school.

On marrying and moving house Mrs Evans clung to the

169

security of her husband and later her home. Mr Evans not only allowed his wife to become dependent but apparently encouraged this by fitting his life-style around his wife's fears. Both partners may have been experiencing considerable secondary gain from this relationship; Mrs Evans fears serving to keep them very close emotionally and physically. Hafner (1982) has argued that in some cases agoraphobia can actually stabilize a relationship as the couple adjust to one another and the constraints of the condition.

Limited in her activities outside of the home, Mrs Evans soon established a pattern of zealous housework and cleaning which allowed her to rationalize her time and prevent her from facing up to the reality of her fears. Eventually however the strain of this pretence became too much and Mrs Evans sought professional help. Medication helped her to increase her repertoire but as the effectiveness of this wore off she regressed again. Eventually, deciding that self-help was the only long-term solution, she sought help again first privately and then through her doctor.

Treatment Procedures

The formulation of Mrs Evans problems was discussed at length in the presence of her husband who quickly came to realize the part he played in maintaining his wife's difficulties. Initially dismissive of the problems, feeling that the couple were 'getting on all right', he gradually began to accept that the lifestyle the couple had taken for granted for sixteen years, was in fact very restricted. At this first treatment session Mr Evans was encouraged to express his fears about his wife becoming more independent, and he required some persuading that improvements in her condition would free them as a couple to pursue new interests and a social life together.

After this initial session with Mr and Mrs Evans, having been assured of their motivation and co-operation with treatment, it was unanimously decided that Mrs Evans be included in an anxiety manangement group. Though initially rather wary, Mrs Evans agreed that this would enable her to face up to her fear of strangers immediately and help her to benefit from meeting new people, each of whom would express similar experiences and symptoms of anxiety as herself. Mr Evans who agreed to act as a co-therapist, was able to learn about his wife's difficulties from the group's handouts, and ensure that his wife was given every support and encouragement to achieve the homework targets set in group.

In view of the longstanding nature of Mrs Evans' problems, and her social isolation, it was important for her to have the opportunity to meet fellow sufferers with anxiety symptoms. Additionally, the group was able to offer support and provided her with an opportunity to test out her fears of people and discover that they were irrational. By the third session of the group Mrs Evans was making excellent progress in her homework tasks to reduce her housework and to address her fears of shopping. Likewise at this session she reported having used public transport for the first time in ten years. She became increasingly confident within the group, enjoying the friendly atmosphere and the reinforcement offered her by other group members for her success.

Just prior to the fifth session of the group Mr Evans telephoned to say that his wife would be unable to attend. Further investigation revealed that the couple had rowed furiously for the first time in their married life, Mr Evans had persuaded her that she need not attend any further, and that if she disobeyed him he would leave her. A meeting with the couple was urgently arranged, just prior to the fifth session of the group, where once more Mr Evans expressed his concern that the marked improvement evident in his wife was forcing them apart as a couple. Though Mrs Evans emphatically denied this, it was clear that her new-found confidence was enabling her to be independent for the first time in their married life. Some time was spent examining the details of Mr Evans' fears. A whole series of irrational and catastrophic ideas were elicited, culminating in Mr Evans seeing his wife drive off into the sunset with another man, whilst he was left helpless and broken, unable to live any longer without her. After much discussion we ended this session by being able to laugh together at these ideas, Mr Evans agreeing how foolish and out of proportion they seemed when analyzed properly.

By the end of this meeting Mr Evans was sufficiently reassured of his wife's commitment to him that he agreed she should complete the anxiety management course. A subsequent meeting was arranged with the couple prior to the sixth session and Mrs Evans' homework targets were deliberately designed to include her husband, consisting of dining out at a quiet, local cafe and going mid-week to the cinema. Mr Evans was delighted at their achieving these targets, and in his enthusiasm he subsequently booked a table at a large restaurant in town. Unfortunately this respresented too large a jump in Mrs Evans' anxiety hierarchy and was fortunately cancelled following gentle persuasion at the next joint meeting with the couple.

Following the eighth and final session of the group Mrs Evans gratefully exchanged telephone numbers and addresses with the other group members. Her questionnaire assessment indicated vast improvements in her condition and these improvements were enthusiastically confirmed by Mr Evans.

At six-month and one year follow-up meetings with Mr and Mrs Evans they indicated her improvements had continued. The couple were planning a holiday with another group member and her husband. They had enjoyed an active and productive social life throughout the past year with other group members and friends from Mr Evans' work. Mr Evans described their relationship as 'perfect, closer than ever'. Mrs Evans was no longer performing her ritualistic cleaning of the house but had taken on a part-time job as a home help which she was thoroughly enjoying.

CASE 4: POST-TRAUMATIC STRESS DISORDER

Referral Letter From a Consultant Psychiatrist

'I would be grateful if you would see this young woman who was very capable and self-assured until involved in a road traffic accident in April. She suffered some neurological damage, which persisted for nearly two months, due to a head injury. She returned to work at the end of June but found that she was too frightened to drive or even to ride as a passenger. She has, with the support of her father managed to tolerate riding as a passenger in a car but recent attempts to take up driving again have resulted in really frightening and quite dangerous panic attacks. She also reports having lost confidence, feeling tense and irritable, and has become socially very introverted.

172

I think that she needs expert help in order for her to rehabilitate herself fully and I would therefore be grateful for your assistance.'

Presenting Problem

This 26-year-old woman, Ms Brown was referred to our department in December some nine months after the original road traffic accident. Ms Brown's memory for the details of the accident was very clear. She was driving her Austin Rover car home from work, mid-afternoon in perfect driving conditions, when suddenly a car pulled out in front of her from a side road. Travelling at around 40 miles per hour she had very litle time to brake and crashed full front into the side of the vehicle pulling out. Ms Brown suffered neurological and physical damage as a result of the accident. The neurological damage persisted for nearly two months and included impaired ability to judge distances, memory problems, and a number of other visual problems including a sensation that solid structures were revolving in front of her. The physical damage was mainly severe strain to her back muscles. The third party involved in the accident admitted liability and was himself uninjured.

Ms Brown's physical rehabilitation did not involve any active treatment but rather required her to remain as motionless as possible for nine weeks. She describes throughout this time having an overdramatic imagination and, as a result of a lack of alternative distraction and occupation, she spent much of this time reliving the horror of her accident.

Following her physical recovery by mid-June Ms Brown returned to work, walking there each morning and being picked up by her father at night. She first attempted to drive again herself whilst on holiday in Wales at the end of June. The only vehicle available to her at that time was her father's Porsche. At her first attempt she found herself completely unable to move the car seemingly being unable to remember how to drive. At her second attempt some days later she was able to drive the car approximately 20 yards and then experienced a severe panic attack and felt unable to continue. She became extremely distressed by these difficulties and it was at this time her father first noticed dramatic mood swings and irritability. Subsequently

173

she did not attempt to drive again at all for approximately four months.

In November of the same year Ms Brown bought herself an Austin Mini in order to teach herself to drive again. With the help of her father she was able to drive short distances in his company. However, any attempt to drive longer distances, over a mile, or to drive alone met with severe and dangerous acute attacks of anxiety.

In addition to Ms Brown's specific driving problems she had also begun to fear going out walking alone at dusk or night time. She lived in the country and described some of the country lanes as racetracks for the local youths. At the root of these problems emerged a fear of being knocked down by one of these reckless drivers. Her mood swings by this time had become more frequent. She described 'sudden patches of blackness' descended upon her and at such times she just needed to be alone. At other times she would pick an argument with her father for no reason and become irritable and aggressive. She had also begun to refuse all social invitations and had taken a number of days off work over the last few weeks. Her sleep was fine, though she experienced occasional nightmares, and there was no change in her appetite or levels of concentration.

At the time of her referral her insurance company were engaged in court proceedings on her behalf for compensation as a result of the accident. 'Compensation neurosis' was considered and discussed as a possible confounding variable in the clinical picture though this was assessed not to be relevant and confirmed by the lack of change in Ms Brown's condition following settlement two weeks after the commencement of therapy.

Background

Prior to her road traffic accident Ms Brown had always apparently been a very capable and self-assured woman. Her father was in diplomatic service and this involved much formal entertaining at the family home. As a child Ms Brown was required to both entertain and socialize with her father's guests. At a young age she was clearly very socially skilled and was confident and mature beyond her years.

Ms Brown's mother died some seven years prior to the

accident, having been ill for some time. Ms Brown played a major role in the process of nursing her mother and though greatly saddened by her mother's death also felt a great sense of relief for her mother, released from the pain of the illness.

Ms Brown described her childhood as very happy. She was an only child and had lived the whole of her life in the same village. She was educated at public school and excelled academically. On leaving school she worked for a time as a secretary in London before joing a local firm of business consultants with whom she was now a senior partner.

Ms Brown lived in a flat near to her father's house. She had held a full driving licence for eight years and in this time she had never been involved in a serious road traffic accident. She was used to using her car daily to commute to and from her work some two miles from her home.

There was no history of anxiety or other psychological problems in Ms Brown or her family prior to the accident.

Assessment Procedures

In addition to the two initial assessment interviews Ms Brown was administered a number of questionnaires including the 'Hospital Anxiety and Depression Scale', the 'Cognitive Anxiety Questionnaire', the 'Fear Inventory', and the 'Effects on Life Inventory'.

The questionnaires offered a picture of both specific and generalized fears relating to traffic with evidence of some depressive symptoms. These problems were markedly affecting Ms Brown's life which had become increasingly restricted by her problems. She was exhibiting a number of patterns of avoidance, most notably using various forms of transport only when absolutely necessary and dramatically reducing her previously hectic social life.

Additionally, Ms Brown admitted to experiencing all of the classic symptoms of an acute attack of anxiety including palpitations, breathlessness, feeling faint and dizzy, sweating, and feeling a need to use the toilet. Such attacks had occurred both in response to attempts to drive but also seemingly out of the blue on two occasions. Though she stated she was fully aware that these symptoms themselves were not harmful she did not really understand them and was very concerned that they made it impossible for her to drive confidently and safely.

Formulation of the Problem

The central factor in the development of Ms Brown's difficulties was obviously the car accident itself. However, it seemed likely that a number of other factors had conspired to intensify her problems necessitating professional help.

Eysenck (1967) has noted that a single paring of a neutral stimulus in a highly intense fear situation can elicit a conditioned fear reaction, in this case to driving. The intensity of this reaction can then increase over time. This effect is known as 'incubation'. As a result of Ms Brown's physical and neurological injury she was required to sit as motionless as possible for a period of nine weeks. During this time her constant reliving of her accident – the highly intense fear situation – served to intensify this fear through this process of incubation. Additionally, during this period and subsequently her fear generalized from her own driving to the driving of others and then to other forms of transport.

Ms Brown was very clearly a self-confident and independent individual who had great difficulty in accepting that she was unable to overcome her difficulties without help. This fact perhaps caused her to initially attempt too much in rehabilitating herself to driving, becoming quickly frustrated with herself and establishing a pattern of severe panic attacks in response to her attempts to drive. This frustration was also manifested in her irritability and mood swings which led to further isolating herself and brooding over her problems. She began to lose confidence through her lack of success and this loss of confidence led to avoidance.

Lastly, perhaps her initial choice to attempt to learn to drive confidently again in a Porsche was unfortunate. The car's driving position, the constriction of space and the potential speed of the vehicle would all make the process of driving more difficult. Driving was obviously not something Ms Brown could take risks with as she felt that her panic attacks made her unsafe to other road users.

Treatment Procedures

Following the initial assessment interviews it seemed important that Ms Brown's father should be engaged in the treatment procedures since he had already cast himself in the role of co-therapist. Initially the couple were offered a full formulation of the development of the problems and a full treatment proposal and rationale. These were accepted unequivocally, Ms Brown being very relieved to understand why her own efforts had failed to overcome the problem and pleased to understand the exact nature and aetiology of her ensuing difficulties, especially her severe panic attack symptoms. She was instructed that the prognosis for these difficulties was good but that rehabilitation would necessarily be a slow and graduated process. Ms Brown felt fully able to accept these facts since she was convinced of the logic of reversing her patterns of avoidance with the graded exposure approach, and she could see how it would lead to a return of confidence and to her full recovery.

Both Ms Brown and her father were taught progressive muscular relaxation exercises. He was asked to encourage her to practice these techniques daily but especially to help her recognize and control feelings of muscle tension and general irritability. Relaxation was also used prior to attempting any behavioural targets and was explained as a process of draining down the stress glass to maximize the likelihood of coping with any further stress. Regular physical exercise was also encouraged as a means of tension release and antidepressant therapy, especially sports allowing social contacts.

It was important that Ms Brown quickly and systematically learned to reverse any avoidance behaviour, so as to stem the generalization of her fears. She was asked not to miss work and to revert gradually to her previous sociability, initially accepting or making one social target each week and gradually increasing this. Though initially lacking some confidence and social interest, she quickly came out of her shell and realized just how much her accident had altered her pattern of life. Her fears of being irritable with her friends were unfounded and she was gradually able to accept lifts on a regular basis both to and from social events from father and friends

As regards Ms Brown's fear of driving, a hierarchy of difficulties was constructed and the process of gradual exposure was likened to the slow but systematic climbing of a ladder. A number of different factors were relevant in constructing these targets, including distance driven, driving accompanied by father, friends or alone, driving a new or well known route, and driving during the day, at dusk or at night. Combining these variables produced sixteen steps, from 'driving with father into and out of the drive of the house' to 'driving along the motorway to Bristol alone at dusk'.

Concurrent with social and driving targets Ms Brown was also gradually reversing her avoidance of public transport. As she achieved more and more and plotted the course of her progress on diary sheets, her confidence gradually returned. Whilst driving herself she occasionally felt it necessary to stop her car where convenient to practise relaxation techniques in order to reduce her anxiety, though generally the pattern of her progress was uncomplicated. She found cognitive techniques of distraction very helpful and found that, if all else failed, singing loudly to herself was an excellent means of distraction and tension release.

Ms Brown took a total of six months to successfully complete all of the sixteen behavioural targets which made up her driving hierarchy. She had reversed all other patterns of avoidance after only ten weeks and her father reported that her mood swings and irritability were no longer evident after a similar time.

In total Ms Brown was seen for ten one-hour therapy sessions, weekly for the first five weeks and then gradually tailing off by mutual agreement. At the one year follow-up she was driving freely and had changed her Austin Mini for a more powerful vehicle without any difficulties. Re-administration of the initial assessment questionnaires indicated neither symptoms of anxiety nor depression at six months and one year follow-up.

CASE 5: WORK STRESS

Referral Letter From Client's General Practitioner

'This 32-year-old man is having problems with anxiety. I believe he is a rather obsessive character who did well in his former job because he was in a very structured environment. He now finds it difficult to set boundaries in his new work environment. I would be grateful if you might consider him for relaxation, problem solving, and assertiveness training.'

Presenting Problem

At the initial assessment interview it soon became clear that Mr Smith's problems were not of recent origin. Indeed, he had changed his job some two and a half years ago. For approximately four years he had been complaining of poor concentration and memory, constant feelings of tension, chest pains on a daily basis, and often had severe headaches lasting most of the day. He had gradually lost all confidence in himself and he had begun to absent himself from work feeling unable to cope.

Mr Smith had undergone numerous specialist medical investigations including cardiology, neurology, and tests of thyroid function. He had in the past taken a number of psychotropic medications including diazepam, lorazepam, amitriptyline, and clomipramine. Over the last year he had taken 20 mg of propranalol daily. Mr Smith had also undergone a private course of hypnotherapy but decided to stop after ten sessions as there was no evident improvement in his condition.

Mr Smith stated that his goal for therapy was to understand his symptoms and eventually eradicate them altogether.

Background Details

Mr Smith was born and bought up in Leeds where he had spent the whole of his life up until his move to work in Reading two and a half years ago. He described his childhood as 'generally happy', though he felt that both he and his younger brother suffered from being over-disciplined by a strict and authoritarian father.

Mr Smith's father was a retired clerical assistant who had suffered four breakdowns with anxiety and depression, the first when Mr Smith was 7 years old. He described his father as a very conscientious man who was unable to refuse any request that people made of him. Despite this generosity to others Mr Smith recalled that his father had little time for his two boys, preferring to spend any spare time that he had reading or wading through a mass of figures for his work at the office.

179

Mr Smith described his mother as a very quiet submissive woman who, though very caring, appeared to find great difficulty in expressing any emotions particularly love for her children. She was a very hard-working woman who left home very early each morning for a cleaning job which helped make ends met financially. In later life Mr Smith's brother had anxiety-related difficulties and had been seeing a psychiatrist. Mr Smith recalled investing much of his childhood in reading books. Though he was a popular child he had only a few close friends. He was sporty at school and enjoyed football, but his greatest prowess was in academic matters. Both his parents were very proud when he carried off the school prize and eventually gained a place at Leeds University, where he read a degree in economics. On leaving university where he once more excelled academically, Mr Smith described rather 'falling into' a job with a large computer marketing firm. Despite his initial lack of vocational preference Mr Smith soon become one of the rising stars of the sales force. He would invariably beat any of the monthly sales targets set for him and was quickly rewarded both financially and with promotion. The work itself was largely office-based, with much transaction over the telephone. Travel within the job was only within the locality.

At this early stage in his career Mr Smith described becoming almost addicted to work. He would start early in the morning, finish late at night, and often spend his weekends at work completing his paperwork. The company was very large and structured and enabled him to see a clear line of promotion ahead of him.

At the age of 27 Mr Smith met, and soon married, a newcomer to the firm. He described his wife as a rather shy but hard-working woman who had ambitions to be a mother rather than a salesperson. Shortly after their marriage Mrs Smith's father died and the couple were forced to move south to Reading in order to be near Mrs Smith's aged and infirm mother. Mr Smith recalls this was the first time in his life that he had been out of Yorkshire, other than for holidays, and he felt very unsure of the move but did not feel he could contradict his wife's wishes.

Mr Smith managed to secure a job near to Reading in a small firm, again in computer marketing. Though initially the requirements of his new job seemed very similar it soon became clear that the structure of the company was very different. Mr Smith described his boss as someone who ran the company more like a happy family than a business. The boss did little work himself, preferring to play golf or spend his day chatting to friends on the phone. Mr Smith very quickly began to settle into his routine of overworking but found that much of his time was spent dealing with work for which his boss had responsibility. Gradually as time went on Mr Smith became the person to whom everyone turned for help and advice as they realized that the company boss, though very pleasant, was uninterested and incompetent. Gradually Mr Smith became more and more overworked, having to extend his long working day even further. Any attempts to discuss matters with his boss were skilfully diffused and made Mr Smith think he was 'making a mountain out of a molehill'.

Shortly after the move Mrs Smith became pregnant. The couple were now beginning to struggle financially, having been unprepared for the high cost of living in the south. With Mrs Smith not working the couple's large mortgage was becoming an increasing strain and the couple were forced to borrow money to meet their debts. Additionally, they described having difficulty getting to know people and feeling very alien and lonely in their new house.

As time went on Mr Smith found work more and more intolerable. He found himself working less and less efficiently, despite putting in increasing numbers of hours. His boss, who was delighted with Mr Smith, was always finding him more work to take on. Mr Smith was aware that he should be looking for another job but described feeling an obligation not to let his company collapse, as he was sure it would if he left. He also reported lacking the confidence to attend interviews. Gradually, as years passed, his physical symptoms become more prominent. Numerous trips to his general practitioner, and various specialist investigations, made little difference, neither did the medication he was offered. Eventually, he began to be terrified of starting work again on Monday mornings. He had sleepless hours each night thinking about work, his financial troubles, and his physical symptoms, which he was sure were indicative of serious physical illness such as a brain tumour and/or a serious heart condition.

Assessment Procedures

Mr Smith was asked to complete initially the 'Hospital Anxiety and Depression' scale and the 'Effects on Life Inventory'. Both these questionnaires produced high scores.

After two further sessions Mr Smith filled out the 'Cooper Job Stress Questionnaire', the 'Type-A Behaviour Scale' and two assertiveness inventories – 'The Gambrill-Richey' (1975) and the 'Rathus Assertiveness Schedule' (1973). Mr Smith described this process as very enlightening and identified with a classical work stress profile of low levels of assertiveness, a high score on the Type-A behaviour inventory, and considerable stress in the job, as measured by 'Cooper's Work Stress Inventory'.

Formulation of the Problem

The objective information derived from the use of question-naires can often be of considerable assistance in confirming a formulation, particularly where there are many different strands of evidence to be considered.

The first part of the formulation of Mr Smith's problems derives from the information obtained concerning his father. Mr Smith's father had had a number of breakdowns diagnosed as anxiety. It is thus possible that Mr Smith may have inherited from his father a biological predisposition towards experiencing severe anxiety when under stress. Additionally, his father, an important role model, appeared to have adopted an over-conscientious approach to his work, having difficulties in setting limits in this, spending all his spare time working. Also, his father had few hobbies and leisure interests with which to relax. Mr Smith may well have learned to live and work in this way himself, through a process of modelling from his father.

Mr Smith's parents apparently offered him little in the way of interaction. From an early age he turned to reading as a means of stimulation and sought to be a high achiever at school, perhaps as a way of being noticed and approved of by his parents. The more he achieved, the greater it seems was the approval and this experience was mirrored in his career. Mr Smith by this time clearly exhibited patterns of behaviour characteristic of Type-A personalities, developing these patterns as a consquence of the reinforcement of parents and work colleagues.

Despite obviously overworking in his first job, Mr Smith did not experience any major physical symptoms of stress until his change of job. At this time he was subjected to a large number of major life changes. He had just got married and very soon after this his wife became pregnant. The couple were then forced to move house, Mr Smith moving for the first time many miles from family and friends. Buying a house and the high cost of living brought financial stress and the couple soon found themselves in debt.

In addition to each of these stresses Mr Smith's new job offered nothing of the structure and reinforcement of his earlier employment. His new boss was only too pleased to let him do all the work and Mr Smith's over-conscientious and hard-working approach simply meant that the more he did the more he was asked to do. In his previous job everyone seemed to know what they were doing and everyone did their own job. Mr Smith had not needed to learn skills of assertiveness with his former colleagues to avoid being put upon, and the lack of these skills with his new boss was costing him dear.

Mr Smith's physical symptoms were his somatic manifestation of stress. Familial inheritance and modelling, stressful life events, Type-A personality characteristics, and chronic lack of assertion all played their part in maintaining and feeding his stress further.

Treatment Procedures

Having derived considerable benefit from the specification of his difficulties using questionnaires, Mr Smith was then instructed in the relationship between stress, anxiety, and physical symptoms. He was much relieved that there was a psychophysiological explanation for his symptoms and that his own assessment of major physical illness was incorrect. Mr Smith quickly understood that his body could be likened to a machine and that any machine can become overstressed if it is not properly cared for. The formulation of his problems was presented to him in full and he made careful note of each point.

The next stage of the treatment was to teach Mr Smith

progressive muscular relaxation. Though clearly there were a number of other factors maintaining his tension and other physical symptoms which needed addressing, relaxation is a skill which takes time to master and is thus often best taught early in the therapeutic process. Having undergone two in vivo training sessions Mr Smith was offered a relaxation tape which he was required to use for daily practice. A tape can often ensure that people exhibiting Type A personality characteristics take their time, rather than rushing the exercises to get on with something else.

At the crux of Mr Smith's problems was clearly the work situation. Mr Smith needed to learn to set limits to his work output and needed to become more assertive with his boss in order to reduce his workload. Having completed the Type A questionnaire Mr Smith had already begun to make changes at work and this was taken to be a sign of motivation and evidence that change was possible. Mr Smith began starting work half an hour later in the morning. Though he was still in long before most of the workforce this was considerable progress. Gradually, he was persuaded to take a lunch-break and then a coffee-break, being sold on the idea of taking care of the body machine. To his delight these reductions in time spent actually working made him work more accurately and more efficiently.

The next skill Mr Smith needed was to become more assertive. This training programme began by teaching him to know and insist upon his rights. He spent much time agonizing over whether he had the right to refuse requests and to deny taking responsibility for other people's problems. More time was spent with Mr Smith discussing some of his irrational beliefs. Specifically his belief that the company would fold without him. He came to realize that though certainly it might be generally less efficient, it had operated for many years before he came and no doubt they would find someone to, partially at least, fill his shoes if necessary. Using role play Mr Smith soon learned to make more demands of his boss. He learned to pass work over and deny any responsibility for other peoples' work, realizing that the more he had taken on the more he was being blamed by his clients for not working on their projects. Additionally, Mr Smith began to delegate work to a junior member of staff and to his secretary. People in the office complained about their new duties and Mr Smith's boss called him in 'for chats' several times, but Mr Smith was not daunted, constantly imagining the scales of stress shifting to balance in favour of his health and happiness, both for himself and, more importantly to him, for his family.

Gradually Mr Smith found his evenings and weekends could be spent enjoying his family life and discovering hobbies and new interests rather than working. He joined a squash club with his wife and quickly began to derive benefit from the physical exercise and began to make friends and socialize more. Mr Smith's physical symptoms also gradually began to reduce. First his sleep improved, his chest pains became less frequent, and, with the aid of exercise and relaxation, he learned to control his muscular tension. By the ninth session Mr Smith was sufficiently confident to 'go it alone', though promised he would phone if he got into difficulties.

At one year follow-up Mr Smith was still continuing to improve daily. Though he still occasionally overworked and got the occasional headache he reported generally enjoying work and his health. Re-administration of Type A and assertiveness questionnaires gave evidence of marked positive changes. Though Mr Smith's boss steadfastly refused to increase his own work output his position within the company was becoming increasingly precarious and Mr Smith was told, unofficially, that he may well be in line for promotion shortly. Mr Smith said he would think about it if the offer came.

REFERENCES

Adams, H. E. (1980) *Abnormal Psychology*, Dubuque, Iowa: Wm. C. Brown Company Publishers.

Alberti, R. and Emmons, M. (1970) *Your Perfect Right: a guide to assertive behaviour*, San Luis Obispo, California: Impact.

Bandura, A. (1969) *Principles of Behaviour Modification*, New York: Holt, Rinehart and Winston.

———— (1977) 'Self-efficacy: towards a unifying theory of behavioural change', *Psychological Review* 84: 191–215.

Beck, A. T. (1976) *Cognitive Therapy and Emotional Disorders*, New York: International Universities Press.

———— (1985) in A. T. Beck and G. Emery (eds) *Anxiety Disorders and Phobias: A Cognitive Perspective*, New York: Basic Books.

Beck, A. T. and Emery, G. (1985) *Anxiety Disorders and Phobias: A Cognitive Perspective*, New York: Basic Books.

Blackburn, I. M. (1986) 'The cognitive revolution: an ongoing evolution', *Behavioural Psychotherapy* 14: 274–7.

Bowlby, J. (1969) *Attachment and Loss. Vol. 1: Attachment*, London: Hogarth Press.

Brandon, S. (1988) 'The classification of anxiety disorders', *Postgraduate Medical Journal* 64, (Suppl.2): 16–21.

Brown, G. W. and Harris, T. (1978) *Social Origins of Depression*, London: Tavistock Publications.

Butler, G. and Mathews, A. (1983) 'Cognitive processes in anxiety', *Advanced Behavioural Research Therapy* 5: 51–63.

Cannon, W. B. (1929) *Bodily Changes in Pain, Hunger, Fear and Rage*, New York: Appleton.

Cassel, J. (1976) 'The contribution of the social environment to host resistance', *American Journal of Epidemiology* 104: 107–23.

Chambless, D. L. and Goldstein, A. J. (1980) 'The treatment of agoraphobia', in A. J. Goldstein and E. B. Foa (eds) *Handbook of Behavioural Interventions. A Clinical Guide*, New York: John Wiley.

Charlesworth, E. A. and Nathan, R. G. (1982) *Stress Management*, London: Souvenir Press.

Clark, D. M. (1986) 'A cognitive approach to panic'. *Behaviour Research and Therapy* 24: 461–70.

Claridge, G. (1985) *Origins of Mental Illness*, Oxford: Basil Blackwell.

Cooper, C. L. (1981) *The Stress Check*, New Jersey: Prentice Hall, Spectrum.

Diagnostic and Statistical Manual of Mental Disorders (1980) Third Edition, Washington DC: American Psychiatric Association.

Diagnostic and Statistical Manual of Mental Disorders (1987) Third Edition, (Revised) Washington DC: American Psychiatric Association.

Dickson, A. (1982) *A Woman in Your Own Right*, London: Quartet Books.

Dryden, W. (1984) *Rational-emotive therapy: Fundamentals and Innovations*, Beckenham: Croom Helm.

Dryden, W. and Golden, W. (eds) (1986) *Cognitive-Behavioural Approaches to Psychotherapy*, London: Harper & Row.

Eayrs, C., Rowan, D., and Harvey, P. (1984) 'Behavioural group training for anxiety management', *Behavioural Psychotherapy* 12: 117–29.

Ellis, A. (1962) *Reason and Emotion in Psychotherapy*, New York: Lyle Stuart.

Ellis, A. (1976) 'The Biological Basis of Human Irrationality', *Journal of Individual Psychology*, 32: 145–68.

Ellis, A. and Grieger, R. (1977) *Handbook of Rational Emotive Therapy*, New York: Springer.

Emery, G. (1985) in A. T. Beck and G. Emery (eds) *Anxiety Disorders and Phobias: A Cognitive Perspective*, New York: Basic Books.

English, H. B. (1929) 'Three cases of the "Conditioned Fear Response"', *Journal of Abnormal and Social Psychology* 34: 221–5.

Eysenck, H. J. (1967) *The Biological Basis of Personality*, Springfield, Ill: Thomas.

French, J. R. P. and Caplan, R. D. (1973) 'Organizational Stress and Individual Strain', in A. J. Marrow (ed.) *The Failure of Success*, New York: Amacom.

Freud, S. (1936) *The Problem of Anxiety*, New York: Norton, first published in 1923 in German.

Friedman, M. D. and Rosenman, R. H. (1974) *Type-A Behaviour and Your Heart*, New York: Knopf.

Gambrill, E. D. and Richey, C. A. (1975) 'An assertion inventory for use in assessment and research', *Behaviour Therapy* 6: 550–61.

Ganster, D. C. and Victor, B. (1988) 'The impact of social support on mental and physical health', *British Journal of Medical Psychology* 61: 3–17.

Gelder, M., Gath, D., and Mayou, R. (1983) *Oxford Textbook of Psychiatry*, Oxford: Oxford University Press.

Goldstein, A. J. and Chambless, D. L. (1978) 'A re-analysis of agoraphobia', *Behaviour Therapy* 9: 47–59.

Hafner, R. J. (1982) 'The marital context of the agoraphobic syndrome', in D. L. Chambless and A. J. Goldstein (eds) *Agoraphobia: Multiple Perspectives on Theory and Treatment*, New York: Wiley.

Hibbert, G. (1984) 'Ideational components of anxiety: their origin and content', *British Journal of Psychiatry* 144: 618–24.

Holmes, T. H. and Rahe, R. H. (1967) 'The social adjustment rating scale', *Journal of Psychosomatic Research* 11: 213–18.

International Classification of Diseases (1975) World Health Organization, Ninth Revision, Geneva, London: HMSO.

Jacobson, E. (1938) *Progressive Relaxation*, Chicago: University of Chicago Press.

Jupp, H. and Dudley, M. (1984) 'Group cognitive anxiety management', *Journal of Advanced Nursing* 9: 573–80.

Johnson, W. (1975) 'Group therapy: A behavioural approach', *Behavioural Therapy* 6: 30–8.

Kendall, P. C. and Hollon, S. D. (1981) *Assessment Strategies for Cognitive–Behavioural Interventions*. London: Academic Press.

Kobasa, S. C. (1982) 'The hardy personality', in G. Sanders and J. Suls (eds) *Social Psychology of Health and Illness*, New Jersey: Lawrence Erlbaum Associates Inc.

Lacey, J. I. (1967) 'Somatic response patterning and stress: some revisions of activation theory', in M. H. Appley and R. Trumball (eds) *Psychological Stress*, New York: McGraw-Hill.

Lang, P. J. (1968) 'Fear reduction and fearful behaviour: a construct', in J. M. Shlien (ed.) *Research in Psychotherapy*, vol. 3, Washington DC: American Psychological Association.

————— (1969) 'The mechanics of desensitization and the laboratory study of fear', in C. M. Franks (ed.) *Behaviour Therapy: Appraisal and Status*, New York: McGraw-Hill.

Lazarus, A. (1976) *Multi–modal Behaviour Therapy*, New York: Springer.

Lazarus, R. S. (1966) *Psychological Stress and the Coping Process*, New York: McGraw-Hill.

————— (1971) 'The concept of stress and disease', in L. Levi (ed.) *Society, Stress and Disease*, vol. 1, London: Oxford University Press.

Ley, R. (1985) 'Agoraphobia, the panic attack and the hyperventilation syndrome', *Clinical Psychology Review* 5: 271–85.

Lindsay, W. R. and Hood, E. H. (1982) 'A cognitive anxiety questionnaire', unpublished, University of Sheffield.

Linsay, W. R., Gamsu, C. V., McLaughlin, E., Hood, E., and Espie, C. (1987) 'A controlled trial of treatments for generalized anxiety', *British Journal of Clinical Psychology* 26: 1, 3–17.

Lynch, J. J. (1977) *The Broken Heart: the medical consquences of loneliness*, New York: Basic Books.

Mathews, A. (1982) 'St. Georges Hospital Anxiety Questionnaire', Unpublished Manuscript, St. Georges Hospital Medical School, University of London.

Marks, I. M. (1970) 'Agoraphobic Syndrome (phobic anxiety state)', *Archives of General Psychiatry* 23: 538–53.

————— (1971) 'Phobic disorders four years after treatment: a prospective follow-up', *British Journal of Psychiatry* 118: 683–8.

Marks, I. M. and Lader, M. (1973) 'Anxiety States (anxiety neurosis): A review', *Journal of Nervous and Mental Disease* 156: 3–18.

Marks, I. M. and Mathews, A. (1979) 'A brief standard self-rating scale for phobic patients', *Behaviour Research and Therapy* 17: 263–7.

Marks, I. M., Gelder, M. G. and Edwards, G. (1968) 'Hypnosis and desensitization for phobias: a controlled prospective trial', *British Journal of Psychiatry* 114: 1263–74.

Marmot, M. G. (1975) 'Epidemiological studies of coronary heart disease and strokes in Japanese men living in Japan, Hawaii, and California,' *American Journal of Epidemiology* 102, 6: 515–25.

Meichenbaum, D. (1974) 'Self-instructional training: a cognitive prosthesis for the ages', *Human Development* 17: 273–80.

Meichenbaum, D. (1975) 'Self-instructional methods', in F. H. Kanfer and A. P. Goldstein (eds) *Helping people change: a textbook of methods*, New York: Pergamon.

Meichenbaum, D. and Cameron, R. (1983) 'Stress innoculation training: towards a general paradigm for training coping skills', in D. Meichenbaum and M. Jaremko (eds) *Stress reduction and prevention*, New York: Plenum.

Mowrer, O. H. (1947) 'On the dual nature of learning a reinterpretation of "Conditioning" and "Problem Solving"', *Harvard Educational Review* 17: 102–48.

Paul, G. L. (1966) *Insight vs Desensitization in Psychotherapy*, Stanford, CA: Stanford University Press.

Powell, T. J. (1987) 'Anxiety management groups in clinical practice: a preliminary report', *Behavioural Psychotherapy* 15: 181–7.

Rachman, S. and Hodgson, R. J. (1980) *Obsessions and Compulsions*, New Jersey: Prentice Hall.

Rathus, S. A. (1973) 'A 30-item schedule of assessing assertive behaviour', *Behaviour Therapy* 4: 398–406.

Salkovskis, P. M. (1988) 'Hyperventilation and anxiety', *Current Opinion in Psychiatry* 1: 76–82.

Sartorius, N., Jablensky, A., Cooper, J. E., and Burke, J. D. (eds) (1988) 'Psychiatric classification an international perspective', *British Journal of Psychiatry*, Supplement 1, vol 152.

Seligman, M. (1971) 'Phobias and preparedenss', *Behaviour Therapy* 2: 307–20.

Selye, H. (1946) 'The general adaptation syndrome and the diseases of adaptation', *Journal of Clinical Endocrinology* 6: 117.

Sheehan, D. V. (1982) 'Current concepts in psychiatry: panic attacks and phobias', *New England Journal of Medicine: Medical Intelligence*, July: 156–8.

Slater, E. and Shields, J. (1969) 'Genetic aspects of anxiety', in M. H. Lader (ed.) *Studies of Anxiety*, Ashford, Headley Brothers.

Smith, M. L. and Glass, G. V. (1977) 'Meta-analysis of psychotherapy outcome studies', *American Psychologist* 32: 752–60.

Smith, M. (1975) *When I Say No, I Feel Guilty*, London: Bantam.

Spielberger, C. D. (1972) 'Anxiety as an emotional state', in C. D.

Spielberger (ed.) *Anxiety: Current Trends in Theory and Research*, vol 1. New York: Academic Press.

Syme, S. L. (1966) 'Sociological approach to the epidemiology of cerebrovascular disease', *Public Health Monograph* 76: 57 63

Thorpe, G. L. and Burns, L. E. (1983) *The Agoraphobic Syndrome*, New York: John Wiley.

Valiant, G. E. (1977) *Adaptation to life: how the best and brightest came of age*, Boston, MA: Little Brown.

Watson, J. B. and Rayner, R. (1920) 'Conditioned Emotional Reactions', *Journal of Experimental Psychology* 3: 1–14.

Westphal, C. (1871–2) 'Die agoraphobie: eine neuropathische erscheinung', *Archiv für Psychiatrie und Nerven Krankheiten* 3: 138–61.

Zigmond, A. S. and Snaith, R. P. (1983) 'The hospital anxiety and depression scale', *Acta Psychiatrica Scandinavica* 67: 361–70.

NAME INDEX

SUBJECT INDEX

acute anxiety spiral 74–5
aggression 21, 36; case study of 160–6
aggressive behaviour 127–8
agoraphobia 26–7, 48, 49; case study
of 166–72; and questionnaire 63;
symptoms of 26–7
alarm reaction 18–19, 70–4; *see also*
fight or flight response
alcoholism 2, 21
American Psychiatric Association's
Diagnostic and Statistical Manual of
Mental Disorders (DSM) 24–5
anxiety: and avoidance 78–9;
behavioural theories of 37–8;
biological theories of 31–4;
cognitive theories of 39–41;
definition of 22–3; diagnosis of 22–
30; and education 64–91; genetic
link in 32–4; and hyperventilation
73; and irrational beliefs 40, 81; and
loss of confidence 79–81; and
maintenance of 77–8; and
management training 48; normal
64–5; and performance 64–5;
psychoanalytical theories of 34–6;
questionnaires 57–63; and self-help
techniques 92–114; self-monitoring
of 55–6; start of 75–6; theoretical
approaches to 30–40; and thinking
81–2; and the three-systems model
23, 44, 49
anxiety management group 141–53;
advantages and disadvantages of
150–1; advice on running 146–9;
characteristics of 141–2;
effectiveness of 152–3; experiences
of 148–9; handouts in 142–3;
homework assignments in 143–4,
148; individuals in 149; programme
for 144–6; role of therapists in 142,
146–9; selection of members of
151–2; therapeutic components of
142–4; use of in case study 170–2
anxiety management training 48, 92–
114; central elements of 64
anxiety states 25, 27
assertive behaviour 111, 128–9
assertiveness 54; case study 184–5;
and communication styles 125–9; in
a group 143, 146, 147; and
philosophy of 124; and
predisposition to stress 14; and
questionnaire 169, 182; rating of
131; training 123–33
assessment 43–63; for anxiety
management group 151–2;
assessment sheet 44–5; and
behavioural symptoms 47–8; of
episodes of anxiety 48–9; and
family background 50; interview
44–55; of mental symptoms 46–7;
of personal history 51; of physical
symptoms 46; of precipitating
stresses 49; of problem areas 84;
theoretical approach to 43–4; *see
also* case studies
avoidance 21; assessment of 48–50,
55; assessment of in groups 145,
147, 153; breaking patterns of 83;
in case study 177; and maintenance
of anxiety 78–82; of panic attacks
72–3; and development of phobia
37; and use of questionnaires 63;
specifying areas of 84